Hypnotherap

For Gavin Emerson, friend and colleague, who has supported and encouraged me at every opportunity and who taught me the beauty and simplicity of hypnotherapy. With grateful thanks.

Hypnotherapy for a better life

Tig Calvert

Hodder Education

338 Euston Road, London NW1 3BH.

Hodder Education is an Hachette UK company.

First published in UK 2011 by Hodder Education.

First published in US 2011 by The McGraw-Hill Companies, Inc.

This edition published 2011.

Copyright © Tig Calvert 2011

The moral rights of the author have been asserted.

Database right Hodder Education (makers)

The *Teach Yourself* name is a registered trademark of Hachette UK.

British Library Cataloguing in Publication Data: a catalogue record
for this title is available from the British Library.

Library of Congress Catalog Card Number: on file.

ISBN 9781444137262

10 9 8 7 6 5 4 3 2 1

www.hoddereducation.co.uk

Typeset by Cenveo Publisher Services.

Printed in Great Britain by CPI Cox & Wyman, Reading.

Also available
in ebook

Contents

Part 2 Self-hypnosis

Part 3 Techniques of self-hypnosis

Part 5   Self-hypnosis for better life-physical well-being

Part 6   Professional hypnotherapy

Meet the author

Welcome to *Hypnotherapy for a Better Life!*

As a psychologist I have always been interested in how we can use our knowledge of how the brain works, and in particular how the mind and body interact, to help people lead happier and more fulfilling lives. I have concentrated my career on investigating the science behind psychological techniques to improve well-being. Hypnosis offers the best therapeutic tool to achieve this. Hypnotherapy is a well-established, scientific, evidence-based therapy which integrates psychology and biology to help people lead happier and more fulfilled lives, as well as being an effective treatment for a range of psychological and physical symptoms. This book brings together scientific evidence and practical techniques to use within self-hypnosis. You often hear statements like 'hypnosis gives you access to your unconscious' and think, but what exactly does that mean? I hope this books explains what this means in biological and psychological terms. I present a neurologically plausible rationale to explain the altered state of hypnosis and the therapeutic value of this altered state.

In one minute

Are you fascinated by the idea of hypnotherapy and how it appears to be able to help people overcome all sorts of deep-rooted problems quickly and effectively? Would you like to find out more about the psychology and science behind hypnosis? Would you like to learn self-hypnosis and specific techniques to help you become a happier and more fulfilled person? Do you want help to overcome issues, such as anxiety, weight problems or sleep issues? Are you interested in how self-hypnosis can help you perform better and be more successful at work, in relationships, in sport or socially? Perhaps you have more serious problems that you feel a professional clinical hypnotherapist may be able to help you with but you don't know enough about the subject to feel confident in booking an appointment? You may even be thinking of embarking on a career as a clinical hypnotherapist yourself, either to complement your existing work in the field of health or education, or as a complete career change, and are keen to know how to go about this. Clinical hypnotherapy is a well-established, scientific, evidence-based therapy which has helped many people to lead more fulfilling and happier lives. In this book you can learn the skills of self-hypnosis to use in your everyday life as well as understanding how hypnosis works and the science behind hypnosis.

Who will benefit from this book?

Hypnotherapy for a Better Life offers a practical introduction to hypnotherapy providing a readable, easy to use educational and self-help book covering the theory and effectiveness of hypnotherapy and self-hypnosis. It provides readers with tools to develop their own skills of self-hypnosis, and information on how they can access hypnotherapy treatment for more severe issues, as well as guidance on professional training for those readers interested in pursuing clinical hypnotherapy as a career. The information in the book is presented in an easy to read format and is based on current scientific understanding and up-to-date neurological and psychological evidence. The biological basis of hypnosis and how it works is discussed in detail. Ethical use of hypnosis is explained and the myths surrounding hypnosis are discussed. It will be of interest to anyone studying hypnosis and self-hypnosis, and will provide an educational tool for psychology students, doctors, nurses, and therapists in training.

Part 1

Hypnotherapy

1

Hypnosis, hypnotherapy and self-hypnosis

In this chapter you will learn:
- *what hypnosis and hypnotherapy are*
- *what hypnosis feels like.*

Hypnosis

Hypnosis is an altered state of consciousness. This altered state of consciousness arises due to changes in the brain. These changes can occur naturally in some circumstances but in hypnosis they are induced with the use of specific techniques. In hypnosis your attention is focused and narrowed. This creates the environment in which your brain can process information in a different way, and allows you to access more areas of your brain. Hypnosis is not a form of sleep, but it has a number of similarities. When you experience hypnosis you often feel extremely relaxed physically, your body may feel as though it has gone to sleep and you often keep very still. In fact you remain awake. The conscious part of the brain is turned down and the unconscious part of the brain is more active.

Hypnotherapy

Hypnosis is the state. Hypnotherapy is the approach. Hypnotherapy is a form of therapy which utilizes the state of hypnosis as its main therapeutic tool. Hypnosis leads to significant changes in mental processes. These changes in the way the brain processes information during hypnosis can be utilized to bring about therapeutic change. Hypnosis allows you to bypass the conscious mind and the limitations of conscious thought. Hypnosis enhances your ability to be imaginative and to process information differently. These abilities are utilized by the therapist to help the client to address problems successfully. Hypnosis has been used as a therapeutic tool for thousands of years but the way hypnosis works has only recently been understood from a scientific point of view.

What is self-hypnosis?

Self-hypnosis involves guiding yourself into this different state of consciousness using specific techniques. Being in a state of hypnosis is beneficial in itself but in self-hypnosis you can also use simple techniques to bring about positive change in your life. Within self-hypnosis you experience deep relaxation and the ability to access and change the way you feel and think about things. It can have powerful effects on psychological and physical issues. We all have internal resources, and self-hypnosis is a way of utilizing these, to achieve happier more fulfilled lives as well as to overcome difficulties. We are born with few fears and no worries or limitations. These develop through experience and learning. Hypnosis allows you to re-learn and change your thinking patterns quickly and effectively.

Insight

The natural state of the body and mind is one of equilibrium or balance. Experiences in life often upset this balance but with hypnosis you can learn to return to a balanced, happy state, free from unnecessary worries or concerns in which you can achieve your full potential.

What does hypnosis feel like?

There is nothing magical about hypnosis, although you may find some of the effects of hypnosis magical in nature. Everyone's experience of hypnosis is unique but there are some common aspects experienced by most people. Hypnosis involves entering an altered state of consciousness. Have you ever been so engrossed in a task, such as playing sport or reading a great novel, that you are completely unaware of what is going on around you and unaware of time passing; you are in the zone? This is similar to the altered state experienced in hypnosis. In other ways hypnosis resembles the experience just before you drift off to sleep, where your mind wanders and you feel very relaxed; you are still aware and yet your body feels asleep. Generally in hypnosis you experience this feeling of deep relaxation, but this is paired by feeling mentally aware. There may be a feeling of detachment from the outside world; for example, in hypnosis you would still be able to hear the traffic outside but it may seem distant and irrelevant. Often people experience some degree of change of sensation in their body, particularly in the limbs. You may experience a feeling of floating, of not quite being aware of your body, of feeling light. Time is often distorted too and it is common to feel that you have been in a trance for only a few moments when actually 20 minutes have passed. Alternatively you may feel you have been relaxed for half an hour and when you look at the clock only a few minutes have passed. It is a pleasant experience.

Seven misconceptions of hypnosis

1 *Hypnosis is magical.*
   Hypnosis is a natural state. There is nothing magical about it.
2 *When experiencing hypnosis you are asleep.*
   When in hypnosis you are generally very relaxed but not asleep. In fact you are in an alert but relaxed state.
3 *Hypnosis is dangerous.*
   Hypnosis itself is not dangerous as it is a completely natural state but it is important to treat it with respect because it is powerful. It is important to use self-hypnosis only with minor issues and never hypnotize anyone else unless you are professionally trained.
4 *In hypnosis you will do things you don't want to do or disclose things you want to keep private.*
   In a state of hypnosis you remain in control and will not say or do anything you do not want to. This misconception arises from stage hypnosis which uses the natural suggestibility of highly

suggestible people to do funny things that they are happy to do. If you notice, stage hypnotists always choose their subjects very carefully. They test people's suggestibility because they know that only very suggestible people will make good subjects for entertainment purposes. Stage hypnosis is very different from the use of hypnosis within hypnotherapy.

5 *There is a danger you will not wake up from hypnosis.*
In hypnosis you are not asleep and you can come out of the altered state at anytime.

6 *Some people cannot by hypnotized.*
Every individual experiences different things when in hypnosis but everyone can, with practice, attain a different state of consciousness. The very elderly and the very young may find it more difficult as their level of concentration may be affected.

7 *In hypnosis you are under someone else's control.*
In hypnosis the person being hypnotized is always in control. You cannot force anyone into hypnosis. In professional clinical hypnotherapy the therapist facilitates the process and helps to produce therapeutic change.

THINGS TO REMEMBER

▶ Hypnosis is an altered state of consciousness.

▶ Self-hypnosis allows you to guide yourself into this altered state of consciousness.

▶ This altered state often involves experiencing a state of deep physical relaxation in which you remain awake.

▶ Hypnotherapy uses hypnosis to bring about therapeutic change.

▶ Within self-hypnosis you can use basis therapeutic techniques to produce positive changes.

▶ These positive changes come about through changing your thoughts and emotional responses.

▶ This can bring about benefits to your general health and well-being.

How hypnosis works

In this chapter you will learn:
- *about the different areas of the human brain*
- *how changes in the brain allow hypnosis to occur.*

The brain and hypnosis

A basic knowledge of brain functioning in relation to hypnosis allows you to understand how it can be used successfully as a therapeutic tool. Changes in the brain create the state of hypnosis and allow for processing of information in a different way. It is this reprocessing that brings about therapeutic change.

This change in brain state comes about due to changes in the autonomic nervous system. There are two main parts to the autonomic nervous system. The first is the sympathetic nervous system, which is dominant when we are aroused, stressed or threatened. Sometimes this is called the 'fight or flight' response. Your heart rate quickens, you sweat more, and your blood pressure increases as your body prepares for action. The second is the parasympathetic nervous system. This is dominant when your body is relaxed. In this state your heart rate slows, your breathing slows and all your bodily functions decrease as your body is in a physically relaxed state. In hypnosis there is a switch to this parasympathetic dominance of the autonomic nervous system, which initiates the altered state of consciousness.

> **Insight**
> The state of hypnosis is not dependent upon one single part of the brain but alterations in many interconnecting systems within the brain.

The following section gives a basic but comprehensive overview of the brain and in particular the structures that are highly relevant to the mechanisms underlying hypnosis and those involved in the production of therapeutic changes when hypnosis is used as a psychological therapy.

The basics of the brain

The brain is the control centre of your body and mind. The human brain has evolved over millions of years but the basic human brain remains similar to the brain of the first humans evolved. The human brain also has many commonalities with animals and others mammals. The main difference is that humans have a more evolved conscious brain. However, the unconscious part of the brain is, in some ways, the more important. As humans we tend to focus on our conscious abilities. Because we have the ability to think in language and communicate with words we tend to over-rely on these abilities. However, most of the processing of the brain goes on in the unconscious part of the brain. The brain processes information from the external world and internal bodily states. Information travels to and from your brain and the rest of your body as nerve impulses along your spinal cord. Through this process the brain regulates conscious and unconscious body processes. It is via these processes that a hypnotic state develops.

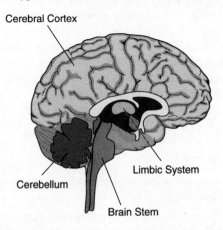

Figure 2.1 The four areas of the brain.

Your brain is made of many parts, each of which has specific functions but the brain also works as a whole. The brain can be divided into three main areas: the cerebral cortex, the limbic region, and the brain stem and cerebellum.

The cerebral cortex

The cerebral cortex is the largest part of your brain, encompassing about two-thirds of the whole brain mass, and is the most recent structure in the history of brain evolution. The cortex forms the outer layer of the brain and it has a heavily folded grey surface. It is responsible for conscious awareness of thoughts and behaviours, and producing and understanding language. The front part of the cortex, the frontal lobe, is specifically involved in conscious awareness in decision making, emotional thought and skilled movements. Behind this is the parietal lobe which perceives and interprets sensations like touch, temperature and pain. At the back of your brain lies the occipital lobe which is concerned with visual images. On either side are the temporal lobes which are involved in hearing and some cognitive processing. You are not aware of the all the processing in the cortex as most of it remains unconscious, but conscious awareness arises from this outer layer of the brain. In hypnosis this conscious part of the brain is less active.

The cerebral cortex is split down the middle into two halves called hemispheres that are joined together and communicate with each other via a massive bundle of nerve fibres called the corpus callosum. Brain activity between the hemispheres changes in hypnosis. Increased activity in the right hemisphere of the brain gives rise to some hypnotic phenomena, such as the dream-like quality of thoughts, increased visual imagery and time perception distortions.

Limbic region

The limbic region lies deep within your brain beneath the middle of your cerebral cortex and on top of your brain stem. It governs the rest of the brain and the body. Its processes are unconscious. This part of the brain processes material before you are aware of it. The limbic system controls the level of activity in the cortex. Signals are sent to the conscious areas of your brain from the limbic region. Alterations in the limbic system are involved in producing the altered state of consciousness experienced during hypnosis. The limbic system also regulates learning, memory, attention and emotions. Changes in the limbic system during hypnosis are also critical to the therapeutic benefit of hypnosis.

Brain stem and cerebellum

The brain stem and the cerebellum monitor most of the basic functioning of the body and are very old in evolutionary terms. They are responsible for regulating many life-support mechanisms, such as your heart rate, blood pressure, digestion, breathing and basic movement. The brain stem is essential in maintaining consciousness. It plays a pivotal role in the altered state of consciousness experienced during hypnosis.

All information relayed from the body to the brain and vice versa, must traverse the brain stem. Pain, temperature and touch are all sensory experiences mediated via the brain stem. These are often altered during hypnosis indicating a change in brain stem activity.

The cerebellum is particularly interesting because it contains more neurons (brain cells) than the rest of the brain put together. It used to be thought that the main role of the cerebellum was to co-ordinate body movements; however, the last 20 years has seen new evidence showing that the cerebellum is also crucial in attention and memory, language and mental imagery. Unlike other areas of the brain which generally communicate in a two-way system the cerebellum tends to send out more signals to the rest of the brain than it receives. During hypnosis changes in the cerebellum are likely to mediate many changes in conscious awareness.

How the brain works as a whole

The brain stem and cerebellum can be viewed as the foundations. They are necessary to human life but are not sufficient for human existence. The limbic region acts as the control centre of human experience. It is unconscious and mediates the activity of the cortex. The cortex allows us to be aware of our human experiences. The limbic region is the most critical part of the brain in hypnosis for two reasons. First, the hypnotic experience comes about because of changes in the limbic system. Second, these changes mediate the therapeutic benefit of hypnosis. Hypnosis is produced by changes in the limbic system and therapeutic change comes about via processes in the limbic system. It contains many important structures including the hypothalamus, the thalamus, the amygdala, the hippocampus, the insula, the nucleus accumbens and the cingulate gyrus. These structures all communicate with each other and also with other widespread areas of the brain including the brain stem and the cortex, as well as the rest of the body.

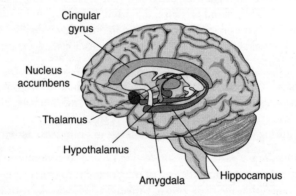

Figure 2.2 The limbic system.

The hypothalamus

The hypothalamus controls much of our everyday functioning. It is a small, almond-shaped structure deep within the limbic system on top of the brain stem. It links many important processes within the body. It regulates body temperature, hunger, thirst, sleep and libido. It has a role to play in emotions and also regulates the immune system.

The hypothalamus is involved in the production of a hypnotic state as it regulates the autonomic nervous system. Changes in the autonomic nervous system, from sympathetic dominance to parasympathetic dominance, are a key feature of hypnosis. This change is regulated by the hypothalamus and plays a major role in producing the altered state of consciousness experienced in hypnosis. The hypothalamus is also involved in the therapeutic benefits of hypnosis. Because of its pivotal role in emotional regulation and mind and body communication, changes in the hypothalamus allow for reprocessing during hypnotherapy.

The thalamus

The thalamus lies just above the hypothalamus and acts as a relay station for information coming into your brain from your senses. It then sends appropriate signals to other parts of the brain. It is involved in the process of inducing a hypnotic trance. Your attention is narrowed and focused when entering a trance state. The thalamus receives less input from the senses and therefore can work in a different way. Alterations in pain perception experienced in hypnosis are also mediated by the thalamus.

The amygdala

The amygdala is known as the fear centre of the brain and is involved in emotional processing. It is responsible for initiating the 'fight or flight' response you experience when faced with danger. It interacts with the hypothalamus, hippocampus and other structures within the limbic region. During hypnosis the amygdala is less active and this contributes to changes in the autonomic nervous system. The body goes into parasympathetic dominance. Your heart rate slows down, your breathing slows and your blood pressure remains low. This produces and sustains the experience of relaxation and the ability of the mind to reprocess thoughts and behaviours. Due to the involvement of the amygdala in emotional processing, changes in this region are also involved in the therapeutic effects of hypnotherapy.

The hippocampus

The hippocampus is a horseshoe shaped layer of cells adjacent to the amygdala. It is responsible for the processing of new memories, emotional regulation and spatial orientation. One role of the hippocampus is to keep the conscious brain attentive. This mechanism is turned down in a hypnotic state. The techniques used to induce a hypnotic state affect the activation levels in the hippocampus. This results in changes throughout the limbic system and the hippocampus appears critical in the neurological mechanism of hypnosis.

Changes in the activation of the hippocampus are involved in the heightened ability to process information in hypnosis. The hippocampus and the amygdala are closely related. Therapeutic change in emotion regulation during hypnosis is facilitated by the links between emotions and memory processed by these two structures.

The insula

The insula is on the outer edge of the limbic region and the inner folds of the cortex. It is involved in conscious awareness. It contains special cells only found in the brains of humans and great apes. The insula is involved in empathy and the ability to preconceive what an experience is going to feel like. It also processes bodily states, for example pain and temperature, and is activated when you think about these states. It is the biological basis of intuition. Along with the hypothalamus and the amygdala it influences the homeostasis of the body, including regulating the balance between the sympathetic and parasympathetic nervous systems, and is therefore involved in the production of a hypnotic state. The insula is also involved in the therapeutic process and in particular the ability to reprocess information using the imagination. The insula plays a part in immune system functioning. Many therapeutic effects experienced with hypnosis are likely to be mediated through the insula.

Nucleus accumbens

The nucleus accumbens, called the pleasure centre of the brain, is involved in reward, pleasure, laugher, sexual arousal, addiction, fear and aggression. It is also involved with what information becomes conscious. It is involved in both the altered state and therapeutic change.

The cingulate gyrus

Resting between the cortex and the limbic region lies the cingulate gyrus. It is situated just above the corpus callosum, the bundle of nerve fibres connecting the two hemispheres of the brain. It is involved in the suppression of cortical activity and the change from conscious to unconscious processing. It also has a wide range of emotional and cognitive functions which influence autonomic activity. It is involved in the emotional response to pain. The anterior cingulate gyrus mediates emotional thoughts and non-verbal communication. It has a major role to play in the therapeutic application of hypnosis.

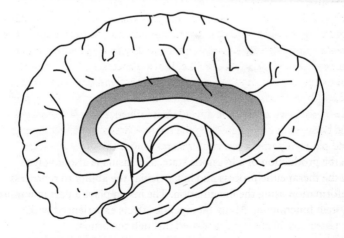

Figure 2.3 The cingulate gyrus.

THINGS TO REMEMBER

► The altered state of consciousness experienced in hypnosis comes about through changes in the brain.

► The brain is composed of three main layers; the brain stem, the limbic region and the cortex.

► Each of these brain areas plays a role in producing the altered state of hypnosis.

► These brain changes also allow for the therapeutic effects of hypnotherapy to be effective.

3

Brain activity and hypnosis

In this chapter you will learn:
* *how hypnosis affects brain waves*
* *how the brain changes in hypnosis affect the body.*

During hypnosis there are changes in the electrical activity of the brain, mediated by the cingulate gyrus. These brain patterns can be measured using electroencephalography (EEG). This involves placing electrodes on the scalp to record the level of electrical activity in the brain. When we are awake and alert, talking to friends or at work, the brain is in an alert state. This is reflected in mainly BETA brain waves which are short and spiky, reflecting lots of activity going on. When we are more relaxed, watching television or listening to music for example, the brain shows slower, more gentle brain waves, called ALPHA waves. When we are asleep the brain is in an even more relaxed state and shows DELTA waves which are much slower, apart from periods of rapid eye movement (REM) sleep when the brain temporarily increases its activity. When a person is experiencing hypnosis the brain takes on a different form, which is neither awake nor asleep but is active but relaxed. The brain in hypnosis produces THETA brain waves. This is the key to hypnosis.

How does hypnosis make the brain work at this different rate?

The techniques used in hypnosis, which will be explained in more detail in the next section, produce this altered state through

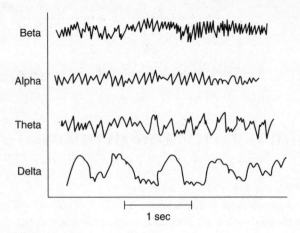

Beta

Alpha

Theta

Delta

|— 1 sec —|

Figure 3.1 Different brain waves.

a number of mechanisms. One of these mechanisms involves changes in the autonomic nervous system. The autonomic nervous system governs the body's state of balance. There are two main parts to the autonomic nervous system, namely the sympathetic nervous system, which is dominant when we are aroused, feeling stressed or threatened. At the other extreme, when your body is relaxed, the parasympathetic nervous system is dominant. In this state your heart rate slows, your breathing slows and all your bodily functions decrease as your body is in a physically relaxed state. Many techniques of hypnosis encourage parasympathetic dominance and this creates a state where your brain more easily produces ALPHA and THETA patterns, which reflect this deeply relaxed state.

The homeostasis, or balance, of the body through the autonomic nervous system is governed by the hypothalamus in conjunction with other areas of the limbic system. The hypothalamus controls the autonomic nervous system through a pathway called the hypothalamic pituitary adrenal (HPA) axis. The hypothalamus sends chemical messages to the pituitary gland, a small structure deep within the brain, which controls the release of hormones. These messages travel down the body to the adrenal glands, situated on top of the kidneys. The adrenal glands then control the level of stress hormones in the body which in turn activates the sympathetic nervous system, which regulates the 'fight or flight' response.

What role does the HPA axis play in hypnosis?

When someone enters into hypnosis they become more relaxed, which sends signals to the HPA axis that there is no danger and it is safe to send messages to the body to go into parasympathetic dominance. This encourages further relaxation and even deeper levels of physical relaxation similar to those which occur during sleep but the advantage is that the person is still awake and has a level of conscious awareness.

How does the mind affect the body?

Traditionally in Western philosophy, the mind and the body were viewed as separate entities, and thoughts were not considered to be able to affect the body. However, with the development of scientific evidence, is it now well established that the mind, thoughts, beliefs and emotions all affect the physical body. Every thought has a neurological consequence. Thoughts affect what is going on in the brain and therefore affect the responses of the whole body.

THINGS TO REMEMBER

▶ The body and mind are connected in a two-way inter-related system.

▶ In hypnosis your brain changes.

▶ In hypnosis the brain is relaxed and shows mainly ALPHA and THETA brain waves.

▶ There is a state of parasympathetic dominance of the nervous system whilst in hypnosis.

▶ This change in body and brain state aids access to the unconscious mind.

▶ In this deeply relaxed state of mind an individual is more open to new ideas and suggestions, as the rational, conscious part of the brain is subdued.

4

....

Unconscious and conscious processing

In this chapter you will learn:
* *the differences between the unconscious mind and the conscious mind*
* *how hypnosis allows you to reach the unconscious part of your mind.*

The conscious and unconscious mind

The brain changes that take place during hypnosis allow you to access parts of your mind that are otherwise non-conscious and inaccessible. The part of the brain which allows you to be aware of your conscious thoughts is just the tip of the iceberg. The unconscious part of the brain is the machine working away behind the scenes. It is vast and holds a reservoir of information.

....
Insight
Have you ever been doing a crossword and found yourself stuck on a clue, only to find that if you leave it and do something else for half an hour, suddenly the answer comes to you? It just pops into your mind. This is an example of your unconscious mind working away and then the answer coming into the conscious part of your brain so that you are aware of it.
....

In fact the majority of brain processing is not conscious; we just feel it is because we are more aware of conscious thoughts. For example, much of what we see and hear is not consciously registered by our brains. It is processed unconsciously, and then some of it reaches conscious awareness.

In both hearing and vision, there are two pathways that process information, a conscious and an unconscious route. The unconscious route processes information very quickly but without fine detail. The conscious pathway is slower but more detailed. We are only aware of the conscious processing. Damage to the conscious visual pathway results in a condition called blindsight. The person cannot consciously see. They are blind. However, they can negotiate around furniture, and if you threw a ball at them that they would reach out to catch it. They would not know why they had suddenly put out their hand because they cannot see the ball but unconsciously they have perceived an object. If shown an emotionally loaded picture people with blindsight will show physical responses indicating perception. This shows that emotion can be, and probably is, processed unconsciously. We have many more emotional reactions than we are aware of.

We also hear things unconsciously. We experience the effects of unconscious hearing in our everyday lives. We are not consciously aware of all the sounds in the room but our unconscious brain is. This is shown in the cocktail party effect. We have all experienced being in a crowded room and being completed focused on a conversation with someone, unaware of the other sounds in the room, until you hear your name. Your unconscious mind was processing all the sounds and when something relevant to you was heard it allowed you to become consciously aware of it.

Other evidence comes from people who have sustained damage to their hippocampus, either through head injury or stroke. The hippocampus, a small section of the limbic region in the brain, is essential in processing new conscious memories. If damaged, the person cannot form new memories and does not remember things for longer than a few minutes. However, if you give them the same puzzle to complete three days running, even though they will not remember completing the puzzle before, they will complete it faster each time. This shows that their unconscious mind was aware that they had completed the puzzle before and learning had taken place. We can learn things without being aware of them.

Another example is visual neglect, where, as a result of specific brain damage, the person has conscious awareness of only half their visual field. Someone with visual neglect will eat only half the food on their plate as they are not consciously aware of the other half. They may dress only half of their body and write only on half a piece of paper. This occurs due to damage to the opposite hemisphere of the brain. Left visual neglect is caused by specific damage to the right hemisphere. The person has no conscious awareness of anything in their left visual field. However, if asked to choose between two drawings of a house, one of which is damaged on the left hand side of the picture, they will choose the undamaged house. They report that both houses looked identical but they unconsciously 'saw' the left hand side of the houses and recognized that one was damaged. They are not aware of why they made the decision. This shows that unconscious processing is not fundamentally different from conscious processing; the difference is that we are not aware of it.

People without brain damage can also be consciously blind. This is called inattentional blindness. In an experiment subjects had to count how many times animated black or white letters bounced against the side of a computer screen. While this was going on a red cross travelled across the middle of the screen. It remained on the screen for 5 seconds. Over a quarter of the people in the experiment failed to notice the red cross even though it was on the screen for 5 seconds. This was because all of their attention was on the black and white letters. This blindness occurs in everyday life but we are not aware of it.

The scientific understanding of brain functioning has progressed enormously in the last few years. It used to be thought that conscious awareness was active and unconscious processing was reflex driven. However, recent evidence suggests otherwise. The biological evidence suggests that there is unconscious brain activity between 100th of a millisecond to 10 seconds before conscious awareness. We become aware of thoughts and behaviours after they have been initiated. Unconscious processes initiate the conscious experience.

Insight

Science may have been limited by old views of the unconscious. People still often talk about the unconscious mind as being somehow different from the brain. The unconscious mind is not some mystical place; it is processes in the unconscious part of the brain.

Differences between unconscious and conscious brain processes

Unconscious	Conscious
Fast	Slow
Rough	Detailed
Unaware	Aware
Non-verbal	Language based
Subcortical (limbic system)	Cortical

Most, if not all, information is processed unconsciously and we only become aware of some information. So what determines whether we consciously become aware of something? This process originates in the unconscious part of the brain. Decisions, thoughts, behaviours, perceptions are all considered in the unconscious mind before you become aware of them.

We have evolved to be on alert for information that is novel, relevant or emotionally charged. New stimulus may be dangerous or offer an exciting opportunity and therefore our brains are on the alert for novelty. Studies have shown that even very small babies focus on new faces more than familiar faces. We are born to notice new things and anything new is much more likely to enter conscious awareness.

Things become conscious when we attend to them. But what dictates what we attend to? The answer to this is probably unconscious processing. For example, relevance plays another important role. We become aware of things that are relevant to ourselves. Have you ever noticed that when you buy a new car you suddenly start seeing more cars of the same make? It is as if suddenly there are more cars just like yours on the road but in fact the number hasn't changed, you just notice them now because they have become relevant to you and therefore come into your conscious awareness.

It is interesting, in the case of inattentional blindness, where people fail to see a red cross on the screen they are looking at, that they always notice if their name appears on the screen. Consciously seeing their name is more likely than consciously seeing the red cross because it is more relevant to them.

Emotions are also mainly unconscious and we only become aware of some of them. The nucleus accumbens, the pleasure centre of the brain, is involved in what becomes conscious, and emotionally relevant things are more likely to become conscious. This is one reason why when you fall in love, you think about that person frequently, and maybe for no conscious reason, you just find yourself thinking about them. Your unconscious brain is sending these messages into your awareness because they are relevant. Emotions are unconscious until they become conscious and we become aware of them.

In normal everyday life, unconscious thinking is passive. You play no active part in it consciously. It controls your conscious thoughts rather than the other way round. However, in an altered state of hypnosis this relationship changes and the flow of information becomes bidirectional.

This is why hypnosis works. Changing conscious thoughts and behaviours is difficult because all thoughts and behaviours originate unconsciously. Therefore being able to tap into this unconscious part of your brain in self-hypnosis allows you to influence what thoughts and behaviours reach your conscious awareness in your everyday life.

So why do we have a conscious and an unconscious mind? Why is some of processing conscious but the majority of it unconscious? Why can't everything just be conscious and then we would be aware of everything? Well that is exactly why. If we were aware of everything we had ever done or thought or felt we would be overwhelmed in our everyday lives. We wouldn't be able to think clearly. That is why only some information enters awareness. A good example of this is learning to drive. You have to consciously think about every movement, from changing gear to steering, to working out when to slow down or when it is safe to overtake. It is mentally draining. However, when you have more experience, many of these things become unconscious; you can do them automatically without having to think about them and this makes the whole experience easier, as you can concentrate on traffic and directions.

Some things that are unconscious can be made conscious at will. For example, breathing is an unconscious process that occurs automatically but you can make yourself aware of your breathing and even consciously change the rate at which you breathe if you wish to. Some things are more difficult to bring into conscious awareness in the everyday waking state but during a hypnotic trance they are much more easily accessible.

Your thoughts and what you think is determined by your unconscious brain. Take the scenario of two people alone in separate houses late at night, just drifting off to sleep. They both hear a noise. One of them thinks; 'that could be someone breaking in', their heart rate starts to quicken and they feel scared. They cannot sleep, and lie awake for an hour feeling anxious. They then find themselves worrying about other things in their lives. The other person hears a noise and thinks: 'I bet that's the wind blowing something outside.' They turn over and drift off to sleep. It has not occurred to them to think it may be something negative. Why? What determines what someone thinks? They haven't chosen consciously what to think of the noise. Their thoughts occur automatically. It may feel as if we have control over our thoughts, but if you analyse it they just appear. This is due to activation within the unconscious part of the brain; in this case, how fired up the limbic system was and in particular the amygdala. If the amygdala is overactive, then this produces anxious thoughts. If the amygdala is calm then calm thoughts preside.

Insight

We put too much emphasis on conscious thought and language. We trust our conscious thoughts too much. If we just realized that they are products and interpretations and not necessarily accurate we would not reinforce them.

Consciousness tries to validate what you implicitly know. Consciousness looks for logical interpretations, but these may not be accurate. The unconscious mind and brain is not inferior and something that needs to be tamed. The conscious brain is an inferior representation of the much more capable unconscious mind. Science has been limited by presuming consciousness is superior just because we are aware of it.

We have all experienced how the brain and its messages can influence our thinking unconsciously. When we are tired or hormonal we can become irritable and all our thoughts seem to be negative. We may even say to ourselves, 'I'm sure I wouldn't normally think that, I must be tired.' But do we ever stop to think what this actually means? Our brains produce different hormones either due to the natural cycle of hormone changes or due to chronic stress or being tired. When our brains change we have different thoughts. We recognize that these thoughts are unusual because we don't normally have them. But actually, all of our thoughts occur due to biological messages in our unconscious brain. The unconscious workings of the brain and in particular the limbic system give rise to conscious thoughts.

Let us carry on thinking about thoughts for a minute. Stop and think how do they arise? And you realize they just do. How many times have you thought or said, 'I wonder what made me think if that?' or 'Why didn't I think of that before?' Even if they are stimulated by an external sensory perception the actual thoughts we have just appear. Our reaction to, and interpretation of, external events is processed via the unconscious part of the brain. Conscious thoughts originate from here. So what is going on in your unconscious brain is the most important aspect of thinking. Trying to alter conscious thoughts with psychological therapies can be useful, but actually effecting change in the unconscious processes can have a much more rapid and long-term effect on thinking and therefore well-being.

Recognizing that you are more than your conscious thoughts allows you to revaluate everything. This opens up possibilities. You are only limited by your consciousness. The unconscious mind is non-verbal and communicates through producing feelings in the body. We can all recognize this – that gut reaction we have to events.

Insight

The physical sensations in the body we experience can give us an indication of how we actually feel about something. Have you ever said, 'it just felt right'? Learning to take notice of these hunches and feelings helps you to be guided by your unconscious mind rather than over-reliance on conscious thought which can be rigid and inflexible.

Spending time in self-hypnosis is actually spending time communicating with your unconscious mind because the outer, conscious part of your brain is subdued and the unconscious, limbic region of your brain is more accessible.

The state of consciousness in hypnosis

During sleep the conscious mind is dormant and the unconscious mind is allowed free rein, which results in dreaming during periods of REM sleep. In hypnosis the conscious mind is less active and the unconscious mind is more prominent than in the waking state.

In other words you get the best of both worlds: access to your unconscious mind, like during sleep, but you remain awake and therefore can become conscious of things otherwise not accessible to you. The brain may be more capable of creating new neural pathways during hypnosis, as it does when we are asleep.

The role of mirror neurons

Mirror neurons are specialized brain cells that exist in many areas of the brain and in particular the insula. Mirror neurons are brain cells that are activated both when we do something and also when we see someone else do something. It is likely that many of the therapeutic benefits of hypnosis occur due to changes in the mirror neuron networks of the brain. Mirror neurons form an unconscious network within the brain. The changes in consciousness during hypnosis produce changes in mirror neurons which lead to brain changes. This allows for the therapeutic changes achieved in a hypnotic state to be evident and beneficial in the everyday life.

Mirror neurons are activated when you deliberately think of something. For example, if I asked you to think of a pineapple. You would form a mental image of a fruit. The same brain cells are activated in exactly the same pattern as when you actually see a pineapple. As far as your brain is concerned, your mind does not know the difference between thinking about the pineapple and actually seeing it in front of you.

Using the imagination whilst in an altered state of hypnosis allows for brain changes to take place because you are forming new memories in the same way you would if you were having those experiences in real life.

We rely on our conscious memory too because we are aware of it. However, it is seldom accurate and sometimes very misleading. A recent study showed that people who watched a video of someone shaking a bottle of pop, often mistakenly thought when asked two weeks later that they had themselves shaken the bottle of pop. They could remember the experience of doing it. Yet this was because their mirror neurons had formed a memory trace of the incident so clearly that it could not be distinguished from a real memory. The more the neural pathway patterns are used, the stronger the mirror neural pathways become, and the stronger the sensations can become.

THINGS TO REMEMBER

▶ The role of unconscious and conscious processing within the brain is altered with self-hypnosis. Most, if not all, conscious thoughts and behaviours originate in the unconscious part of the brain. We feel that we have control over our thoughts because we are aware of them only when they become conscious. It is, however, the unconscious part of our brain that decides what we think and therefore, being able to access this part of the brain in self-hypnosis allows us to influence our conscious thoughts in everyday life, to increase well-being. We are more than just our conscious thoughts.

Part 2
Self-
hypnosis

5

....

What is self-hypnosis?

In this chapter you will learn:
* *some of the the uses and benefits of self-hypnosis.*

Self-hypnosis involves guiding yourself into an altered state of consciousness. When in this altered state you can use techniques to improve your well-being and then, when you are ready, you can return to an everyday conscious state.

Establishing an altered state of consciousness

↓

Utilising the altered state of consciousness

↓

Re-establishing an everyday conscious state

Figure 5.1 Self-hypnosis process.

There are many benefits to self-hypnosis. Some people choose to use self-hypnosis because they want to be able to manage their emotions, while others are simply curious. Many benefits come from purely spending time in this unique state. Practising regular self-hypnosis has benefits due to the physiological changes that occur. Following regular self-hypnosis people frequently report feeling more alert, emotionally calmer and able to perform at a higher level in their everyday lives.

Uses of self-hypnosis

Many people choose to practise self-hypnosis for self-development in areas such as self-esteem, motivation, confidence and creativity. An increase in positivity and mood is commonly experienced following hypnosis and this is strengthened with repeated periods of hypnosis. Self-hypnosis is particularly useful in addressing stress-related problems. Regular self-hypnosis has been shown to reduce stress and anxiety. Stress has a negative effect on the body and in particular on the immune system. Self-hypnosis can therefore be useful in maintaining a healthy body and mind.

Self-hypnosis can also be used as a self-help therapy, using techniques to address specific issues, such as weight problems. More severe psychological and physical issues require the experience of a professionally trained clinical hypnotherapist. In some instances it may be appropriate to consult a professional clinical hypnotherapist in the first instance and then progress to using self-hypnosis. How to find a professional hypnotherapist is covered in the latter section of this book.

The psychology of hypnosis

Hypnosis allows you to enter a state where the usual limitations, particularly in thinking, are removed and you can easily 'think outside the box'. This is due to being able to access the whole of your mind, not just your conscious thoughts. We are often limited by thoughts and beliefs in the conscious mind because they are rigid and inflexible. For example, in a conscious state people are limited by their beliefs about their age, their abilities and their level of confidence. These self-limiting beliefs are more easily challenged in hypnosis as the critical, conscious part of the brain is not as dominant.

How does self-hypnosis help with everyday problems?

Self-hypnosis can help you achieve positive well-being in three major ways:

1 Entering a state of parasympathetic dominance allows for your body to rebalance and counteracts some of the physical consequences of stress.
2 Entering into a state of self-hypnosis allows your mind to come up with new and creative solutions through the unconscious parts of the brain being more accessible.
3 Positive states of mind can easily be reinforced during self-hypnosis to enable you to feel happier in your everyday life. Therefore issues, if difficult to change at the present time, can be less problematic.

Simply entering into a state of self-hypnosis is therapeutic in itself. It allows the body and mind a window of opportunity to reprocess information and rebalance the chemicals and hormones surging through our bodies at any one time. The feelings of deep relaxation that accompany self-hypnosis are very pleasant. Often people experience many benefits through practising self-hypnosis without any formal therapeutic techniques.

Insight

Purely entering a hypnotic state is beneficial. However, once you are more experienced you may wish to use some basic techniques while you are in self-hypnosis to work on specific issues in your life.

Negative thinking or behaviour is often the result of a lack of processing or biased processing, which makes negative thoughts more likely to enter consciousness. The old adage that time is a great healer is true because with time the brain naturally processes information so it becomes less poignant, and therefore you are less aware of it. When this mechanism fails either due to habitual reintegration of the negative feeling or due to some blockage then the memory or emotion remains raw and does not lose its potency. Hypnosis allows for the reprocessing of emotions. That is why you can experience rapid and effective relief from issues that have been a problem for months or even years.

THINGS TO REMEMBER

▶ Self-hypnosis involves creating an altered state of consciousness.

▶ This altered state of consciousness can be utilized for therapeutic benefits.

▶ You can then benefit from these changes when you re-establish an everyday alert state of consciousness.

6

Practical aspects of self-hypnosis

In this chapter you will learn:
- *techniques for self-hypnosis*
- *the answers to some frequently asked questions*
- *the physical and perceptual changes you may experience in self-hypnosis.*

Self-hypnosis is easy to learn and is an enjoyable experience. It is important to practise self-hypnosis, as you will find it becomes much easier with practice.

Insight

When first using self-hypnosis you may find that you drift into a wonderfully deep state of relaxation and feel so relaxed that you find it hard to continue playing any active role in the process. This is fine. You will benefit from being in that state and sometimes this is all you need. As you develop your skills and experience you will find to easier to control the process.

There is no reason why anyone cannot become skilled at self-hypnosis if they are motivated and dedicate time to practise the techniques. It is often useful to establish a routine, setting aside a time and some space for you to concentrate. Most people initially find it easiest to practise self-hypnosis in a quiet place, either sitting comfortably or lying down. There is a chance in the beginning that you may fall asleep if you lie down but with practice this will be less likely. However, if you are wishing to use self-hypnosis to help you to get to sleep then it is fine to do it in bed lying down and then you can drift off to sleep afterwards without disturbing yourself!

The key to a successful experience is to allow whatever naturally occurs to develop. For some people this will be clearly evident but for others more subtle changes will occur initially.

Imagery and visualization

Visualization is a skill used in self-hypnosis. Often people worry that they are not very good at visualization but it is a natural skill all people have and will come quite easily in hypnosis. We have all experienced daydreaming and even though we are discouraged as children to daydream, actually daydreaming is a very good way of letting the mind process information. Our bodies and mind are governed by circadian rhythms throughout the day that have peaks and troughs of concentration. Down time is essential for processing.

Not all imagery is visual and it may be that you are more inclined towards one of the other senses – kinesthetic (touch), hearing, smell and even taste. You can develop your skills with all forms of imagery, using all the senses with practice. All imagery is individual to you. When you read a novel you will naturally create an idea in your own mind of what the characters look like and the buildings and scenery within the novel. Have you ever watched a film recreating a book you have previously read? Did the characters look like you thought? Often it is quite disturbing if they don't look anything like the image you have created and sometimes they capture your image really well. The images we create without consciously doing so are a good example of visual imagery. It comes quite naturally, and you may not even realize you do this. It is part of why reading a book can be so engrossing and being deeply engrossed in a novel is a similar experience to a hypnotic state.

Goal setting

If you wish to use self-hypnosis to help you make specific positive changes in your life it is useful to consider what you want to achieve. Be specific in your desires. It is important to be realistic but also to stretch yourself and to be ambitious in your goals. It is a good idea to keep a diary of your experiences to record your progress and to reflect on your development both in terms of your skills in self-hypnosis and the issues you are working on.

Sat 8th Oct

Self-hypnosis

Really enjoyed practising today. Noticed I felt so relaxed and 'different' – everything seemed to slow down.

Positive changes I want to make

I worked on feeling more confident. I want to be able to speak in meetings without going red and shaking.

Thoughts

Feeling that I have much more energy since using self-hypnosis and really enjoying being able to relax as well. I'm getting the hang of it and it's really exciting. I've got a meeting next week so I'm going to use it specifically for that and visualize myself feeling calm in the meeting.

Figure 6.1 Example of a diary page.

Frequently asked questions

How long should I spend in self-hypnosis?

Essentially you can spend as long as you want practising hypnosis. To start with it may take you 10–20 minutes to achieve an altered state but this will become easier and quicker with time and practice. Most people then choose to spend 30–40 minutes in this state, but it is not essential to spend this long. You can benefit from brief episodes of self-hypnosis. If you do not bring yourself out of hypnosis after about 40 minutes your mind will probably wander and you will naturally come out of the state or you may drift off to sleep. With practice you will be able to have more control over this process.

What if I am distracted?
When learning and practising self-hypnosis, to allow yourself to relax fully and enjoy the experience as much as possible, it is best to try to reduce the number of distractions. Turn your phone off, go somewhere quiet and ask other people in the house not to disturb you. However, if you need to attend to something urgent you can easily and safely come out of your self-induced hypnotic state at any time.

If there are distractions that you do not have to attend to, such as sirens in the background, street noise or a telephone ringing that doesn't need answering by you, then you can easily incorporate these distractions into your trance and use them to deepen your experience even further. For example, you can think 'all the noises in the background just remind me how far away they are and how deeply engrossed I am that I don't even need to worry about them … they just encourage me to relax even deeper'. When you have developed your skills you will find that you can easily enter a state of self-hypnosis virtually anywhere, even in noisy environments with others around you.

How do I know if am in hypnosis?
Hypnosis is a different experience for different people but there are signs you can look for that you have achieved a state of self-hypnosis. Often time is distorted so it may feel as if you have been in an altered state for an hour when it's only been a few minutes, or you may feel it's been a few minutes when its actually been an hour. You may also notice that your body responds to suggestions of physical sensation like feelings of warmth or heaviness, heat or coldness, which is a good indication that you have achieved a good level of hypnosis. Do not worry about how deep you feel your state is. It will become easier with time to deepen your experience, and beneficial effects can be achieved from being in a very light hypnotic state.

Below is a list of changes you may notice that are an indication that you have achieved an altered state of consciousness and are in a state of self-hypnosis.

Indicators of achieving an altered state of consciousness in self-hypnosis

PHYSIOLOGICAL CHANGES

There are a number of physical changes you may experience. These are an indication of an altered state, but remember that you will not necessarily experience all of these. Any of these can indicate to you that you have successfully achieved a different state.

Flickering eyelids and rapid eye movements – changes in the electrical activity in your brain result in natural changes in eye movements. Your eyelids may flicker or you may find your eyes darting around, similar to the rapid eye movements that accompany dreaming experienced during sleep.

Change in respiratory rate – you may notice that your breathing becomes slower and you naturally breathe more deeply. This is an indication that your body has entered parasympathetic dominance.

Involuntary muscle twitching (myoclonic jerk) – this is very common. You may notice your fingers twitching or your legs jerking. You may have experienced similar twitches in your muscles just before you drop off to sleep. This occurs in hypnosis as your body goes into parasympathetic dominance.

Tingling in hands and fingers – changes occur in your body when in parasympathetic dominance that may cause numbness in extremities or tingling sensations in your limbs, especially your hands and feet.

Heaviness in limbs – you may notice a change in the feelings in your body. For example your legs and arms, and even your whole body, may feel heavy, as if they are sinking into the chair or bed you are lying or sitting on.

Feeling of lightness – while some people experience a feeling of heaviness in the body, others may experience a feeling of lightness. You may experience both of these at different times.

Lethargy – you may feel tired and feel that you can't be bothered to do anything. This is a clear indication that your body has entered parasympathetic dominance.

Drifting – there may be a change in temporal orientation with regards to time and place which is often accompanied by a feeling of floating.

Involuntary rocking of the body – if you are sitting, you may find yourself gently rocking. This is normal physiological occurrence related to brain hemisphere changes.

Slumping – if you are sitting, you may notice your body slumping. Don't worry, you will not fall off the chair but your shoulders may slump as your body relaxes.

Head dropping – in a similar way it is common for your head to drop if you are in a seated position.

Changes in salivation – this can cause an increase in the swallowing reflex or sometimes dribbling. This is normal and is an indication that your body is in a deeply relaxed state. This is partly due to the physical changes as your jaw drops when deeply relaxed. Physiologically the body produces more saliva when relaxed. You may have noticed the opposite effect to this when you have been in a state of high anxiety where you experienced a dry mouth.

Flattening of physical facial features – often you may become aware that your facial features flatten out. This is a common phenomenon when your body is in a deeply relaxed state.

Light snoring – changes in your breathing and relaxation of the facial muscles can result in light snoring. This is not an indication that you are asleep and you may be aware of the snoring. It is a normal physiological response.

Immobilization – it is common to experience the feeling that you can't move. In fact you can move if you desire, but in an altered state of consciousness the messages from the brain to the body are slower and the body is less responsive. You may find you remain still, without moving, for quite long periods of time. You will have little desire to move.

Suspension of the cough reflex – often the normal reflexes of the body also relax and if you have a cough you may find you experience a suspension of the desire to cough.

Eyes watering – you may notice your eyes watering.

Stomach rumbling – in parasympathetic dominance the internal organs also relax and you may be aware of your stomach rumbling as an indication of this.

PERCEPTUAL CHANGES

You may also be aware of changes in your perceptions. Some of your perceptions may change to become more heightened initially and then may become reduced as you progress.

Perception of sound – initially you may experience a heightened perception of sound, for example the clock ticking may appear very loud. At other times you may not notice any sounds around you as you are completely absorbed in your own experience.

Feeling an itch – you may become aware of having an itch. However, due to the physiological changes experiences you may find you can't be bothered to scratch your itch and it will just go away.

Becoming aware of own heart beat – you may become more aware of your own heart beat and feel it and hear it within your body. This is due to the perceptual changes in your body as you become immersed in your own existence.

Heightened imagination – your imagination becomes much more vivid due to the hemisphere changes in the brain.

Increased awareness of fragrances – accompanying the increase in your ability to use your imagination you may experience an increased awareness of fragrances, either real or imagined.

Enhanced ability to perceive colour – in a similar way colours and sounds in your imagination may be enhanced and appear more vivid and real than usual.

Time distortion – this is very common. This is a clear indication that you have been in an altered state of consciousness as time perception is tied to conscious awareness.

Reduced awareness of physical sensations – you may experience a reduced perception of physical sensation. Accompanying this you may have a loss of awareness of bodily position. Your body may feel asleep while your mind remains alert.

Feeling that you can't open your eyes – it is common to feel that you can't physically open your eyes. This is due to your eyes actually rolling back in their sockets when very physically relaxed and in a state of parasympathetic dominance. In fact, if you needed to you could open your eyes.

A suspension of normal physical needs – in a waking state the body makes you aware of basic bodily needs like thirst or hunger. In self-hypnosis these signals are suspended and you may not notice feeling thirsty or hungry until you return to a normal waking state.

Dream-like state – you may experience a dream like state where your imagination seems to take on a role of its own and your mind drifts from one image or thought to another quite naturally. This is due to higher activation in the right hemisphere of your brain.

Reduced anxiety – any feeling of anxiety may be reduced as your conscious brain is subdued. You may notice a feeling of calmness. When in parasympathetic dominance fewer stress chemicals are produced by the body and therefore you feel calmer.

Feeling of detachment – you may notice a sense of detachment from thoughts and bodily sensations.

Spontaneous recall of pleasant memories – because the conscious part of your brain is less active, you may notice that you suddenly remember a pleasant or happy memory from the past that you have not thought of for a long time. This is due to the subtle brain changes that take place.

Enhanced feeling of well-being – you are likely to experience at some point a feeling of enhanced well-being, of feeling happy and content, and you may even feel that you want to smile or laugh.

THINGS TO REMEMBER

► Self-hypnosis is easy to learn.

► Self-hypnosis is a pleasurable experience.

► Everyone's experience of hypnosis is different.

► Deep relaxation is commonly experienced.

► There are many subtle signs that indicate a state of hypnosis.

Part 3
Techniques of self-hypnosis

7

....

The process of self-hypnosis

In this chapter you will learn:
- *some techniques to begin the process of achieving self-hypnosis*
- *some precautions to take.*

The following chapters will guide you through the process of self-hypnosis. Each step is explained and examples are provided to help you to develop your skills in self-hypnosis.

Establishing an altered state of consciousness

Establishing an altered state often involves focusing your attention and producing a state of relaxation. It may involve using your imagination and inner voice to communicate with yourself. This encourages parasympathetic dominance of the autonomic nervous system which initiates changes in the brain which produce the state of hypnosis.

A variety of techniques to establish a state of self-hypnosis are provided. Each uses a different sensory modality or experience to facilitate an altered state of consciousness. Providing different methods allows you to experiment with different techniques to find the one that suits you best. It also allows you to vary the way you enter self-hypnosis. You can use a number of different techniques in succession. This enables you to create a more pronounced experience. The techniques all conclude with you allowing your mind to drift to a pleasant place. This allows for your body and mind to remain in this altered state and you will benefit from experiencing this state without the need to focus on specific changes. Purely spending time in self-hypnosis has many benefits. Subsequent chapters focus on specific psychological techniques that can be used within self-hypnosis to promote well-being.

Pleasant place

At the end of each technique you allow your mind to drift to a pleasant place. One of the beautiful aspects of self-hypnosis is that in self-hypnosis you can create a special place where you can escape whenever you feel the need. The process involves building an image of a place you choose. It can be anywhere. It can be somewhere you know or can be entirely fictitious, based on your imagination. Often it is a mixture of the two.

> **Insight**
> I personally like to enter my special place through a concealed doorway in an old wall surrounding by climbing roses. This image is based on my early memories of the book *The Secret Garden* which as a child I found magical and exciting. Even now if I see an old wall which resembles what I imagine the *Secret Garden* wall to look like it makes me smile.

The advantage to having a special place is that it allows you to deepen your experience easily by just entering that special place. It also gives you somewhere where you feel completely safe and secure, where you can engage in a deeper relationship with yourself.

Your special place can be anywhere but it is best to create somewhere tranquil and calming. It can be a room or garden, beach or wooden hut high in the mountains, a tree house, or a posh hotel room; anywhere, in fact. There may be occasions within self-hypnosis when you wish to experience thrill seeking activities and imagine somewhere much more daring but for this exercise try to create somewhere you feel safe.

This special place can also be used as an access point to your unconscious mind. Your unconscious mind is fundamentally different from your conscious mind. In a sense your consciousness and the thoughts in your conscious mind are socially constructed. They are judgmental, based on beliefs, and are often rigid. The unconscious mind is not limited by these conditions and is more accepting, non-judgmental, without any of the socially constructed limitations placed on you in the real world.

Once you have created this special place you can access it at any time, either within self-hypnosis or as an addition to self-hypnosis in your everyday life, for example as a brief escape prior to an important presentation at work.

Techniques

Each technique for achieving self-hypnosis is described in detail and the procedure is explained. Where appropriate a script is provided. These scripts are designed as a guide. It is not necessary that you follow the script word for word, although if you prefer to record yourself reading the scripts and entering hypnosis through listening to your own recordings this is fine. Read the explanation and then read through the script a couple of times so that you get a feeling of what it is designed to achieve. Following each script the main points are highlighted to allow to you guide yourself easily through the process. Your inner voice should be soft and unhurried and leave pauses (shown as ...... in scripts). This allows you to process the information fully and naturally deepens your state.

Concluding your period of self-hypnosis and returning to a normal alert state is described. Before you start you may want to decide how long you want to spend in hypnosis and you will find that you naturally come out of the state after this period of time. If you are concerned that you may drift off to sleep and need to ensure that you don't, then set an alarm, but put it somewhere in the distance so that it will not startle you. When you hear the alarm in the distance you can bring yourself back to a normal state of alert awareness with the technique described.

You may want to remove your shoes and loosen any clothing that may constrict you. Make sure you are warm enough as when your body goes into a state of relaxation your body temperature naturally falls. Once you are comfortable, close your eyes and use one of the techniques given below to enter into self-hypnosis.

The techniques taught in this section are designed to be used in self-hypnosis. Do not attempt to hypnotize others unless you are fully and professionally trained. Exploring self-hypnosis is often a starting point for people interested in the subject and if you become interested in professional training as a clinical hypnotherapist details are given in later sections.

Do not use self-hypnosis whilst under the influence of alcohol or recreational drugs and do not use if driving or operating equipment.

Do not use any form of self-hypnosis is you suffer from a mental health disorder, and always consult your doctor if you are unsure.

THINGS TO REMEMBER

► Establishing an altered state often involves focusing your attention and producing a state of relaxation.

► It may involve using your imagination and inner voice to communicate with yourself.

► A number of techniques can be used to establish the state of hypnosis.

8

Physiological techniques

In this chapter you will learn:
• *how to use physiological feedback to produce a hypnotic state.*

Some techniques use the sensations in your own body to focus attention and produce the hypnotic state. This technique uses the natural physical responses of the body to reinforce the change in brain state. You will notice that the script refers to processes that you naturally experience in hypnosis, like feelings of heaviness. Through the imagination, these physical experiences are used within the visual scenes you are creating. This feedback response reinforces and enhances the physical changes in your brain and body which produce the altered state.

Physiological feedback using visualization

This technique involves imagining a state of relaxation and using the power of your imagination to produce physical relaxation. Imagining an experience initiates a physical response in the body. The part of the brain that is central to this process, the insula, reacts as it would if you were actually experiencing the occurrence you are imagining. This natural feedback system produces a deep state of physical relaxation. The body goes into a state of parasympathetic dominance and you enter a state of self-hypnosis.

Using this technique you imagine being somewhere in nature, on a warm summer day, and imagine the warmth of the sun of your body. You may like to think back to a time on holiday or imagine what it would be like to be on one of the gorgeous white beaches you may only ever have seen in pictures. Using your imagination, you direct the warmth of the sun down your body. Starting with your face, relax every muscle in your face as you imagine the sun's warmth infiltrating all the muscles in your face, progressing down your whole body. Close your eyes and breathe through your nose.

Script for physiological feedback technique

As I gently close my eyes and focus on my breathing, in ...... and out ...... and while I continue to focus on my breathing I realize there is nothing of importance for me to do ...... just to be ...... this is my time ...... a time just for me ...... a time for me to really concentrate on myself ...... I am just going to let myself focus on my favourite place in nature ...... and it's a beautiful day ...... I notice the sky is a special shade of blue, very clear ...... it's a warm day ...... a warm summer's day ...... there is a dazzling sun in the sky ...... and ...... it's so bright that I just want to relax and enjoying feeling the warmth of the sun on my body ...... and surprisingly I find that I can direct the sun's rays over my body, and as I realize this, I begin to direct the light from the sun over my face ...... I can see its light as a golden stream of bright yellow and orange ...... and I can feel the warmth of the light from the sun on my face ...... just relaxing those muscles across my forehead ...... drifting down around the eyes and the nose and mouth ...... and as I do this ...... I find that the facial muscles begin to flatten out as they relax ...... and I let go ...... all the way ...... as the warmth spreads down into my jaw ...... letting go of any tension ......

And it's a beautiful day ...... I move the light from the sun into my neck ...... feeling the warmth of the sun over my neck, relaxing all those muscles, letting go ...... as the sunlight moves down across my shoulders I feel my shoulders letting go of any tension ...... like a weight has been lifted off them ...... I realize how relaxed I feel ...... so comfortable and at peace with the world ...... all of my attention focused on the warm feelings of relaxation spreading down through my body ...... and as I direct the light from the sun down my right arm ...... seeing ...... feeling the warmth of the sun ...... the glow from the orange beam of light ...... down from the shoulders to the

tips of the fingers ...... the right arm begins to relax and let go ......
relax and let go ...... and it's a beautiful feeling to be here right now
...... the warmth of the light from the sun penetrates the nerves and
bones and muscles of that right arm all the way through ...... it is
such a beautiful day ...... as I move the sun over to my left arm and
guide the light from the sun down the left arm ...... from the top of
the shoulders all the way down to the tips of the fingers ...... I can
feel the left arm relaxing ...... becoming heavy ...... and comfortable
and relaxed ...... now the light moves across and into the chest area
and the chest and all the muscles there relax ...... my breathing
deepens quite naturally ...... slow deep breathing ...... without effort
...... and the relaxation continues down into my abdomen ...... and
all the way down to my hips and thighs and over to the right leg
...... the beautiful warmth of the sun sinks all the way down the leg
...... relaxing every muscle ...... down to my toes ...... all the way
down the left leg from the top of the hips all the way down to the tips
of my toes ...... I just let go of any tension ...... and it's a beautiful
day ...... I am now only aware of how my body feels ...... totally
and completely relaxed ...... from the top of my head to the tips of
my toes ...... and as I become less aware of my body ...... I realize
that I can just forget my physical body ...... as I notice that I am not
fully aware of all of my body ...... as it rests so peacefully ...... and I
can just forget about it ...... and I can just rest here and as my mind
relaxes even further I just notice the sun in the sky going down as
the day comes to an end ...... with the sun going down ...... further
down in the sky ...... deeper and deeper ...... and the sky is ablaze
with an abundance of colours of crimson and bright purple and blue
and yellow streaks ...... and it's a beautiful evening ...... and the
sun goes further and further down ...... over the horizon, until ......
all that is left ...... is a black ...... velvety sky ...... and twinkling
up there in the sky is a single shining star ...... and I find myself
completely engrossed in that one star ...... nothing else matters
except this beautiful single solitary sparkling star in the sky ...... and
it's a beautiful night ...... apart from the one star it is very dark, but I
feel so safe ...... so comfortable ...... so relaxed ...... and calm ......
as I find myself moving towards that star in the sky ...... moving
up ...... and up and up ...... my body feels weightless as it lifts up
to the star ...... going higher and higher, up and up ...... and as the
star grows bigger and bigger I realize I am getting quite close to the
star ...... closer to its beauty and light ...... as it just gets bigger and

bigger ...... brighter and brighter ...... until all at once I am that star in the night sky ...... that beautiful star ...... twinkling away ...... that silver solitary star in the night sky ...... I become the star and the star is me ...... and it's a beautiful star ...... and I find myself drifting deeper and deeper ...... becoming even more deeply relaxed ...... just letting go ...... deeper and deeper ...... into an inner peace ...... as I allow my mind to drift to a special place of comfort ...... as I imagine my perfect place ...... my special place ...... a pleasant place ...... where I can just be ......

MAIN POINTS

▶ Imagine lying relaxing in the sun.
▶ Imagine the warmth of the sun travelling down your body.
▶ Imagine every part of your body relaxing in turn.
▶ Imagine the sun setting in the sky and it becoming night.
▶ Imagine a single star in the sky getting nearer and brighter.
▶ Imagine you and the star integrating.
▶ Allow your mind to drift to a pleasant place.

THINGS TO REMEMBER

▶ Physiological techniques allow you to develop an altered state of hypnosis through the natural feedback responses of the body. With the use of your imagination and self-communication your natural physical responses are reinforced and enhanced which produces the altered state.

9

Physical techniques

In this chapter you will learn:
• *a physical technique, the raised arm technique.*

Physical techniques use physical movement to induce a different state. The movement is often very subtle and it is paired with communication of physical relaxation. Physical techniques are useful as you can condition the altered state to a physical movement and enter into this different state easily.

Raised arm technique

This technique combines gentle physical movement of your arm lowering with evolving feelings of relaxation. It focuses your attention internally, and the physical movement, in this case your arm lowering, corresponds with the changing mental state. In this technique you raise your arm to eye level in front of you and focus all of your attention on your outstretched hand. Centre your visual attention on your hand, looking at all the physical features of the hand. Allow all of your sensory perception to concentrate on the sensations and feelings in your hand as you look at it. After a few moments close your eyes and, keeping your hand out in front of you, continue to imagine the image of your hand in your mind. Communicate sensations of relaxation and heaviness. As you let your hand naturally descend down into your lap or onto the bed you communicate to the rest of your body that it is relaxing ever more deeply.

Script for raised arm technique

As I become comfortable and raise my arm out in front of me ...... I begin to focus on my hand ...... I notice the colour and texture of my skin ...... and I see the whole of my hand just resting there in front of me ...... and I focus all of my attention of my hand ...... and begin to notice the sensations in my hand ...... the temperature ...... the feelings ...... and I can just allow my eyes to close and they rest comfortably ...... I can still see the image of that hand ...... so still ...... there in front of me ...... and as I continue to focus all of my attention on the feelings and sensations in my hand ...... as it just rests there in front of me ...... I begin to notice the sensations in my hand changing ...... my hand is getting heavier and heavier ...... as it begins to slowly drift down ...... I notice a wave of relaxation spreading down my body ...... all the way down my face ...... and as that hand slowly drifts down so I notice a feeling a relaxation spreading all the way down my neck ...... as my whole body relaxes all the way ...... my hand ...... feeling so heavy now ...... slowly continues to drift down ...... as my body lets go ...... and the relaxation spreads down into my shoulders ...... relaxing even more deeply ...... letting go of any unnecessary tension ...... as my hand drifts further down ...... and my body continues to let go ...... and I can just allow my body to continue to relax ...... all the way down over my chest and abdomen ...... relaxing all the way down my back ...... with my whole arm now feeling heavy and tired ...... and I can allow it to sink down slowly ...... any tension melting away ...... as the wave of relaxation drifts down my legs ...... all the way down ...... to my ankles ...... my feet ...... my toes ...... and I don't even need to take any notice of my body now ...... as my arm is becoming heavier now and drifts down ...... all the way down ...... and comes to rest ...... and my hand can just rest as I allow my mind to drift to a pleasant place ......

MAIN POINTS

- ▶ Hold your arm out in front of you at eye level.
- ▶ Focus all of your attention on your outstretched hand.
- ▶ Close your eyes and picture your hand in your mind.
- ▶ Communicate feelings of heaviness and relaxation.
- ▶ Allow the arm to drift down gently.
- ▶ Communicate relaxation spreading down through your body as your arm drifts down.
- ▶ Allow your mind to drift to a pleasant place.

THINGS TO REMEMBER

▶ Physical techniques allow you to use physical movement of the body to centre your attention and coupled with communication of deep relaxation produce the altered state of self-hypnosis.

10

....

Sensory techniques

In this chapter you will learn:
* *two sensory techniques, the hot air balloon technique and the pool immersion technique.*

With sensory techniques you use your sensory imagination to establish an altered state of consciousness. This can involve all the senses, visual, auditory, touch, smell and taste. This focused attention on sensory experiences encourages the production of ALPHA brain waves. The conscious part of your brain becomes less active and the body goes into a state of parasympathetic dominance. Visualization also creates a physiological response related to the activity you are visualizing. Therefore, to induce hypnosis it is beneficial to visualize activities that correspond to this state.

Hot air balloon technique

In the first technique described here you use the image of a hot air balloon rising up into the sky. When using a visualization technique you initially control your imagination. You can imagine being alone or with other people. Let your imagination create the scene in as much detail as you can. Use all of your senses. Imagine what the ground feels like underfoot. Can you feel the slight breeze from the wind on your face? Are there any aromas? What sounds can you imagine? As you begin to enter hypnosis you may notice that your imagination takes over, creating a dream-like state. Your unconscious mind is involved in creating the experience and the creative part of your mind is more active. You will notice subtle changes in your bodily sensations as you begin to feel lighter and lighter. You may notice your breathing becoming naturally slower and a feeling of tingling or numbness in your hands and feet, extending to your arms and legs and then your whole body.

Script for balloon sensory technique

As I make myself comfortable and rest my eyes ...... I focus on the feelings in my body and just allow myself to let go of any tension ...... and as I focus on my breathing ...... quite naturally ...... I just notice my breathing naturally deepens ...... as I notice relaxing further with each breath ...... and I can use my imagination to allow this relaxation to continue even further ...... and I begin to imagine ...... being out in the countryside ...... walking down a footpath to a gate ...... and the gate opens onto a field ...... and I can open the gate and walk into the field ...... as I look around the field ...... seeing the soft green grass ...... and feeling the breeze on my face ...... looking up to the sky above ...... noticing the colour ...... a clear blue sky ...... with just the occasional white fluffy cloud ...... I glance over and standing there in the middle of a field is a hot air balloon ...... and as I imagine walking over to the hot air balloon ...... I imagine the feel of the ground underfoot ...... and as I get nearer I notice the sound of the flames ...... see them soaring high above the basket ...... it's quite a magnificent sight ...... the basket ...... resting on the ground ...... so strong and stable ...... as I notice the smell of the wicker as I walk up and touch the sturdy basket ...... knowing that I can climb inside and go on an exciting journey ...... and inside the basket it is comfortable ...... with seats and cushions ...... and I can create a comfortable space for myself ...... feeling safe and secure ...... and there above me the hot air from the flames above rises up into the balloon ...... and as the balloon begins to rise gently and slowly ...... I can see the balloon high above ...... filling up with warm air ...... just gently gliding upwards ...... away from the normal hustle and bustle of the world ...... into the quiet space in the sky ...... and as I notice my breathing ...... breathing quite naturally ...... and as I breathe in and out ...... with every in-breath I imagine that the hot air balloon is rising ...... gently ascending higher and higher ...... and with every out-breath I notice I am letting go of any tension ...... allowing myself to feel and enjoy the experience ...... and as the balloon rises higher and higher ...... I notice that I feel lighter and lighter ...... as if my whole body is floating ...... and I can just let the balloon glide as high as it chooses to go ...... high up into the sky ...... above the trees ...... above the houses ...... I can look down and see the houses and streets, fields and rivers below me ...... so small and insignificant ...... and with each and every breath, as I drift higher and higher ...... feeling lighter and lighter ...... my imagination takes me on a journey as I just enjoy this wonderful feeling of lightness, of freedom ...... and I can go wherever I choose ...... to my special place ...... a pleasant place ......

MAIN POINTS

- ▶ Imagine standing in a field.
- ▶ Imagine a hot air balloon.
- ▶ Climb into the hot air balloon and be aware of it rising up into the sky.
- ▶ Allow the hot air balloon to drift off into the sky.
- ▶ Communicate feelings of lightness.
- ▶ Allow your mind to drift to a pleasant place.

Pool sensory technique

A second sensory technique involves creating the sensory experience of your body becoming submersed in warm water. This creates a state of relaxation partly through conditioning as your body may already associate warm water with a positive relaxed state. All senses can be involved, feeling the sensation of warm water against your skin, hearing the sounds of the water, smelling the aroma, observing the colours of the water. Obviously if you find water is not to your liking then choose an alternative method.

Script for pool sensory technique

As I allow myself to consider the possibility of just being ...... not having to do anything ...... I can just be ...... and as I consider this possibility I can just allow my eyes to close ...... and I can imagine there ...... in front of me ...... a beautiful pool with crystal clear water ...... as I notice the colours and shapes rippling gently across the surface of the pool …… it looks so inviting …… and as I imagine just dipping my toe into the water …… and I feel the water against my skin …… I realize it is beautifully warm …… soft against my skin …… as I step into the pool and feel the warm water caressing my ankles …… and as the warm water rises up …… as I step deeper into the pool I notice that my body is beginning to feel so relaxed …… as the warm water covers my lower legs …… my legs feel so pleasantly relaxed …… and these feelings of relaxation in my legs …… continue to travel up my body as the warm water envelops my lower body …… over my knees …… up to my thighs …… and my legs feel warm …… and so deeply relaxed …… as all the unnecessary tension just drifts out of my body …… as my muscles let go of any tension …… as it just melts away……and as I glide even deeper into the warm water and the water drifts up to my waist …… and then I sink even deeper in the water up to my chest and back …… and as I submerse my hands in the water and then my arms …… and I can just allow myself to lie back in the warm water …… floating quite naturally …… and I am surprised at how easy it is just to let go and let my body float effortlessly in the water …… so deeply relaxed all through my body …… and with every in-breath I breathe in feelings of calmness …… and serenity …… and with every out-breath …… as I allow myself to float …… feeling so deeply relaxed and comfortable …… and I let my mind drift to a special place.

MAIN POINTS

▶ Imagine a warm pool of water.
▶ Imagine stepping into the pool.
▶ Communicate feelings of relaxation spreading through your body as you immerse your body in the water up to your chest.
▶ Lie back and float in the warm water.
▶ Allow your mind to drift to a special place.

THINGS TO REMEMBER

► Sensory techniques use your sensory imagination to establish an altered state of consciousness. This can involve all the senses, visual, auditory, touch, smell and taste. This focused attention on sensory experiences encourages the conscious part of your brain to become less active and the body goes into a state of parasympathetic dominance.

11

....

Breathing techniques

In this chapter you will learn:
• *a breathing technique.*

If you are particularly stressed or find relaxing has been hard in the past you may wish to use a breathing technique to help you relax fully. You may use a breathing technique in conjunction with other techniques to enhance your ability to achieve an altered state. Concentrating on your breathing and focusing on slow, deep breathing is an excellent way of entering into a deep state of relaxation that can induce hypnosis. Often people breathe quite rapidly and take very shallow breaths, from the top of their lungs, rather than breathing through their stomach. This is a learned behaviour and becomes habitual. It can occur because you are feeling stressed and anxious but can also exacerbate these feelings of anxiety. If you watch a baby or small child breathe, their stomach naturally rises up and down with each breath. This is the natural and healthy way to breathe.

Using your breathing is an excellent way of producing physiological changes that naturally induce relaxation. When you are anxious or stressed your breathing naturally quickens. This is because your hypothalamus has sent chemical messages to your pituitary gland, and from there to your adrenal cortex to produce stress chemicals, like cortisol. This is your 'fight or flight' response. Controlling your breathing so that you breathe more slowly and deeply encourages your brain to send messages to the same parts of the brain and body that it doesn't need to produce stress hormones, that everything is fine, that you are safe and well and your body goes into a state of parasympathetic dominance. Deep breathing triggers a relaxation response in the body. Your breathing will then naturally deepen more, your heart rate will decrease and your blood pressure will stay low. You are setting up a positive set of messages that affect your whole body and mind. The other advantage of focusing on your breathing is that it encourages you to focus on your internal experience. This is useful in hypnosis.

Breathing technique

Always breathe through your nose. This prevents hyperventilation. Do not force the breath, be natural and relaxed in your breathing. Do not over-breathe. You often hear that it is important to count to five on your in-breath and ten on your out-breath. This is not advised. Everyone naturally breathes at a different rate and if you force yourself to breathe too slowly this can actually be counterproductive. Don't put any pressure on yourself to breathe too deeply or too slowly, just allow yourself to breathe at a pace that is natural to you. The breath should be one smooth sequence. Do not deliberately hold your breath. When your breathing deepens you may notice you naturally pause before needing to breathe in again. This is a natural relaxation response. If you get light-headed you may be trying to breathe too deeply. In this technique you reinforce the state of relaxation with self-communication of relaxation.

Script for smooth breathing technique

As I just settle myself down ...... and allow myself some time ...... some time just for me ...... some time just for me to be ...... and there is nothing of any importance I have to do ...... I can just be ...... and the thought of having some space and time for me ...... for me to concentrate on myself ...... allows me to let go of any thoughts about the outside world ...... as I allow my eyes to close ...... and I consider that although breathing is an unconscious process ...... I can have control over my breathing ...... and having control over my breathing allows me to change the way I feel ...... and I allow myself to consider how I would like to feel ...... relaxed and calm ...... and so I can direct these feelings as I begin to notice and control the way I breathe ...... quite naturally ...... as I don't have to force anything ...... I can just notice breathing in through my nose ...... slowly and smoothly ...... and as I do I hear myself saying the word *calm* ...... as I breathe in calmness ...... and as I do I let my whole chest and abdomen fill up with air ...... as my whole body and mind feel calm ...... and then naturally just allow all the air to leave my body as I exhale through my nose ...... slowly and smoothly ...... and as I do I hear myself saying the word *relaxed* ...... as I can just let go ...... and let my body and mind relax all the way through ...... as I expel all the air out of my body ...... and I can just pause until my body indicates to me to breathe in ...... and as I do so ...... breathing slowly and smoothly in through my nose ...... and hearing silently the word *calm* ...... as I breath in calmness ...... letting my chest and stomach rise ...... filling my body with calmness ...... and then just let it go ...... exhaling slowly and smoothly ...... hearing silently the word ...... *relaxed* ...... as on each out-breath I feel more and more relaxed ...... just letting go ...... and I can continue to just concentrate on my breathing as I naturally breathe slowly and smoothly ...... breathing in feelings of calm, and on every out-breath experiencing relaxation spreading down through my body ...... and as I continue to breathe slowly and smoothly I can just allow my mind to drift to a pleasant place ...... a special place ...... where I can just allow myself to relax and feel calm ...... where I can forget about the outside world and relax as deeply as I choose to ...... as I drift to a pleasant place ......

MAIN POINTS

▶ Inhale slowly and smoothly and silently say the word 'calm'.
▶ Allow your stomach to rise until you are full of air.
▶ Do not hold your breath.
▶ Exhale slowly and smoothly through your nose and silently say the word 'relaxed'.
▶ Expel all the air out of your lungs and repeat.
▶ Continue for as long as you choose.
▶ Allow your mind to drift to a pleasant place.

THINGS TO REMEMBER

▶ Concentrating on your breathing encourages you to develop a state of relaxation quite naturally. Breathing techniques can be used in conjunction with other techniques to enhance relaxation.

12

Eye fixation techniques

In this chapter you will learn:
* *an eye fixation technique for inducing a relaxed and focused state.*

Eye fixation technique

Narrowing your focused attention is one way a change in state can be achieved. In this technique you focus all of your attention on a specific point. Concentration and this focused attention encourage your brain waves to slow down and an altered state of hypnosis to occur.

Eye fixation involves keeping your eyes open and fixed on a specific target. You can choose a point above eye level, perhaps on the ceiling above you or the corner of the room. Keep your head still and lift your eyes to look up at this point. It is important to choose a point to focus on that is above eye level and to keep your head still, thereby encouraging your eyes to look upwards at the point you have chosen. When in a state of relaxation your eyes naturally move upwards, and deliberately keeping your eyes in this position sends messages to your brain that you are becoming more relaxed. You will notice that as you stare at that fixed point, your vision becomes blurred, your eyelids begin to twitch and your blinking rate increases. You may find your eyes begin to defocus naturally. That's fine, just allow it to happen. As you allow this process to continue and as you continue to focus fully on the fixed point, your eyes will begin to feel heavy and tired. You may have a strong desire to close your eyes. At this point allow your eyes to gently close and continue to communicate suggestions of relaxation. If you are sitting up you may also find your shoulders and head begin to drop as you become more relaxed. Alternatively you can choose to focus on anything in your visual field. You may like to light a candle and focus on its flame; if you are sitting in front of a real fire you can focus on the flames in the fire. This is a beautiful way of entering self-hypnosis. If you choose to practise self-hypnosis outside then you can focus on a flower or a tree or even a blade of grass. In this case you don't raise your eyes but just fully focus on whatever you have chosen to focus on and immerse yourself in the experience until you naturally want to close your eyes. It is not essential to close your eyes at all and you may remain with your eyes open and still achieve an altered state. This is common in daydreaming.

Script for eye fixation technique

As I sit (or lie) here comfortably and focus all my attention on the point I have chosen ...... I find it easy to narrow my attention ...... just to focus on that point ...... looking at it intently and immersing myself into the experience ...... and as I do ...... I begin to notice subtle changes ...... changes in colour ...... my vision may change ...... becoming blurred ...... I may notice that I begin to blink more rapidly ...... as I let my eyes rest on that point ...... I notice that the muscles around my eyes are beginning to relax ...... and as I try to keep my eyes open ...... I feel they want to close ...... my eyelids are becoming heavy and tired ...... I notice this feeling of heaviness spreading all around my eyes ...... even down to the rest of my face ...... and I continue to focus all of my attention ...... I notice my vision becoming fuzzy ...... misty ...... defocused ...... and I begin to notice my breathing is naturally becoming slower ...... slow and deep ...... and with every breath my whole body seems even more heavy and relaxed ...... and each blink of my eyes becomes slower and slower as the eyelids seem to rest for a moment before opening again ...... with each breath my eyelids become heavier and heavier ...... until I feel I can no longer keep my eyes open ...... I close my eyes ...... and I feel so deeply relaxed ...... still and calm ...... as I continue to see that point I have been focusing on in my mind's eye ...... as it feels so good to close my eyes ...... allowing my whole body just to relax all the way through ...... with each breath ...... relaxing deeper and deeper ...... all the way ...... deeper and deeper

...... I am aware that there is nothing of any importance for me to do ...... just be ...... I can allow my body just to drift ...... and allow my mind to drift ...... to a special place ...... to a pleasant place ......

MAIN POINTS

▶ Choose a point above eye level to focus on.
▶ Keep your head still and lift your eyes to focus on the point you have chosen.
▶ Continue to focus all of your attention on that point.
▶ Communicate feelings of relaxation.
▶ Notice your blinking rate increasing and your eyelids becoming heavy.
▶ Allow your eyes to close.
▶ Allow your mind to drift to a pleasant place.

THINGS TO REMEMBER

▶ Eye techniques offer a way of inducing a relaxed, focused state that evoke neurological and physiological changes that produce a relaxation response in the body and an altered state of consciousness.

13

....

Numerical techniques

In this chapter you will learn:
• *several numerical techniques for entering a state of self-hypnosis.*

Counting down is a very effective method of altering your state of awareness and entering self-hypnosis. Counting is methodical and involves little conscious effort as numbers are so familiar. This focuses the brain's attention but also allows the brain to change from conscious processing to unconscious processing. There are various methods. These techniques can be used alone or to accompany any of the other techniques described.

Verbal counting technique

Some people find that using a verbal technique is the easiest way for them to enter into a state of self-hypnosis. In this technique you combine counting backwards from 100 and verbally suggesting deep relaxation. You initially start by counting and saying phrases out loud. You then proceed to saying them silently to yourself as you begin to change your level of awareness to an internal focus.

Sitting or lying comfortably, begin by allowing yourself to focus fully on the physical sensations in your body. Close your eyes and become aware of your breathing. Always breathe in and out through your nose. There is no need to alter your breathing. Begin to count down slowly, out loud, from 100. After each number say, out loud, the words 'deeply relaxed'. For example 100 deeply relaxed ...... 99 deeply relaxed ...... 98 deeply relaxed ...... 97 deeply relaxed 96

deeply relaxed …… continuing as long as you choose. You will notice that it takes more and more effort to continue to say the numbers and each time you say *deeply relaxed* your body receives signals from your brain to relax even further. You will continue to say the numbers and the words 'deeply relaxed' until your mind becomes so relaxed that you simply forget to speak and you can drift deeper and deeper into a state of deep relaxation and allow your mind to drift.

Script for verbal counting technique

As I make myself comfortable and relish the idea of having some time to myself …… I can close my eyes and as I do so …… I can switch off from the outside world …… and as I prepare to allow myself to just relax …… to enjoy a state of deep relaxation …… and so as I notice my breathing and notice noticing my breathing …… I can begin to count down every time I breathe out …… 100 deeply relaxed …… 99 deeply relaxed …… 98 deeply relaxed …… 97 deeply relaxed …… 96 deeply relaxed …… I count slowly down …… becoming more and more relaxed with each number …… 95 deeply relaxed …… 94 deeply relaxed …… 93 deeply relaxed …… 92 deeply relaxed …… 91 deeply relaxed …… 90 deeply relaxed …… 89 deeply relaxed …… 88 deeply relaxed …… 87 deeply relaxed …… and I wonder how long it will take me to relax so fully that I no longer say the numbers and words out loud …… as I continue silently in my head …… 86 deeply relaxed …… 85 deeply relaxed …… 84 deeply relaxed …… 83 deeply relaxed …… 82 deeply relaxed …… 81 deeply relaxed …… 80 deeply relaxed …… 79 deeply relaxed …… 78 deeply relaxed …… and I wonder how long it will take me to relax so fully that I no longer say the numbers and words at all …… I just forget …… and I am so deeply relaxed that I can allow my mind to drift …… to drift to a special place …… a pleasant place ……

MAIN POINTS
▶ Count down from 100 out loud.
▶ After each number say the words 'deeply relaxed'.
▶ At any point change to counting silently to yourself and continue to say the phrase 'deeply relaxed' silently.
▶ Allow your mind to drift to a pleasant place.

Numerical techniques with imagery

You can combine counting down with imagery. In this technique you use the numbers 10 to 1 and you do not say the numbers out loud but instead silently in your head. You combine counting down with a visual image of going down. There are two alternatives given here, walking down a set of stairs and going down in a lift. The combination of counting down and imagining going down involves multiple sensory experiences. These physiological changes alter brain waves, establishing a state of parasympathetic dominance and causing changes in hemispheric processing. Always count backwards, down from 10 to 1, rather than forwards, 1 to 10. This is because the human mind naturally associates counting backwards with going down.

Stairs count down technique

As I focus on my breathing ...... in and out ...... just slowing down with each breath ...... and I can just lie (or sit) here ...... enjoying a bit of time for me ...... some space for me ...... just to relax ...... and I can allow my imagination to drift ...... as I imagine I am standing at the top of a beautiful staircase ...... and I can imagine the stairs in front of me ...... stretching down ...... I can feel the banister as my hand rests upon it ...... and I feel safe and secure ...... standing at the top of this staircase ...... and my mind imagines where the staircase is taking me to ...... to a place where I feel safe and comfortable ...... relaxed ...... into my own inner world ...... where I feel completely comfortable ...... and in a moment I am going to walk down the stairs, one step at a time ...... and with each step down the stairs ...... I will notice that I feel more and more relaxed ...... allowing myself to go deeper and deeper into a beautiful state of deep relaxation and hypnosis ...... I will begin to count down from 10 to 1 and with each descending number I will take one step down the stairs ...... with each descending number I will find myself becoming one tenth or ten per cent even more absorbed ...... with each descending number and each step down the stairs I will feel more and more deeply relaxed ...... (*begin counting down slowly and silently from 10 to 1 and imagine yourself walking down the stairs, one step at a time*) 10 ......

9 ...... and with each step down I allow myself to drift deeper ......
8 ...... deeper and deeper ...... 7 ...... as very pleasant sensations of
safety and comfort spread down through my body ...... 6 ...... with
every breath just letting go ...... 5 ...... deeper and deeper still ......
4 ...... and I notice as I go down the stairs how detached I feel....
entering into my own world ...... 3 ...... 2 ...... all the way down
into my special place ...... a place just for me ...... where I feel safe
and secure ...... happy and relaxed ...... all the way down ......
deeper and deeper ...... 1 ...... and as I reach the bottom step ......
and step off I can continue to allow myself to drift even deeper ......
as deeply as I choose to go ...... all the way ...... as deep as I choose
...... (*pause here and just allow yourself to be experience whatever
occurs*) and I can allow myself to drift just as deeply as I wish ......
imagining what it would be like to go down past 1 ...... down to 0
...... and even down into minus numbers ...... all the way ...... down
to minus 1 ...... minus 5 ...... minus 10 ...... even down to ......
minus 50 ...... minus 100 ...... as my mind can take me on a special
journey wherever it wants me to go ...... to a special place ...... all
the way ...... deeper and deeper ...... to a pleasant place ......

MAIN POINTS

▶ Prepare to walk down the stairs and suggest physical relaxation.
▶ Imagine walking down stairs.
▶ Count down from 10 to 1 as you imagine walking slowly down
  the stairs.
▶ Continue to imagine counting down into minus numbers.
▶ Allow your mind to drift to a pleasant place.

Lift count down technique

The lift technique involves imagining you are in a lift and you can
control the descent of the lift. This allows changes to take place
in your sensory perception, thus enhancing a state of hypnosis.
Obviously, if you find enclosed spaces are not to your liking then
choose an alternative method.

Lift count down script

As I close my eyes ...... and allow myself to consider how pleasant it is ...... just to rest my eyes ...... and allow myself to experience a time of quiet ...... a quiet time just for me ...... and I can allow my imagination to take me on a journey ...... I see a door in front of me ...... the door to a lift ...... and I press the button to call the lift ...... I imagine where the lift could take me ...... on a journey deep inside my mind ...... into my unconscious mind ...... to a place where I feel totally calm and relaxed ...... to a place where I feel safe and secure ...... and as the lift arrives and I hear the sound of the doors opening I look inside the lift ...... as the doors gently open ...... and I notice how warm and comfortable it looks inside ...... and I walk into the lift and look around ...... I notice a dial with numbers lit up from 10 to 0 ...... I press the button indicating 0 and as the doors close gently in front of me ...... I enjoy the feeling of shutting out the external world ...... enjoying this special journey down into my special world ...... feeling comfortable and safe ...... and as the lift begins to move down ...... as the numbers descend ...... as each floor passes ...... I am aware of drifting deeper and deeper ...... feeling more and more comfortable ...... as the numbers descend ...... 10 ...... 9 ...... 8 ...... 7 ...... with each floor passing allowing me to relax even further ...... 6 ...... 5 ...... 4 ...... as the lift moves smoothly down ...... 3 ...... 2 ...... 1 ...... all the way down past 1 to floor 0 ...... and as the lift gently rests at floor 0 ...... and the door slowly opens ...... I can take a step out into a beautiful place in my imagination ...... wherever I choose to go ...... feeling so deeply relaxed and comfortable ...... and drift to a pleasant place ......

MAIN POINTS

- ▶ Imagine a lift door opening and enter the lift.
- ▶ Imagine the lift descending and suggest physical relaxation.
- ▶ Slowly descend in the lift.
- ▶ As the door opens at the bottom floor allow your mind to drift to a pleasant place.

Numerical technique with physical relaxation

An alternative way of entering into a different state involves integrating counting down with physical relaxation. In this technique you imagine each part of your body in turn relaxing more deeply as you count down from 10 to 1, thus producing a rapid relaxation response through muscle relaxation paired with the conditioned numerical response. Starting with your head and face communicate relaxation and begin counting down from 10. Each descending number corresponds to a part of the body as you communicate relaxation all the way down the body. Number 9 corresponds to the neck, 8 corresponds to the shoulders, 7 corresponds to the arms, hands and fingers, 6 corresponds to the back, 5 corresponds to the chest and abdomen, 4 corresponds to the hips, 3 corresponds to the thighs and knees, 2 corresponds to the lower leg, and 1 corresponds to the ankles, feet and toes.

Script for count down with relaxation technique

As I enjoy allowing myself some time ...... just to relax ...... and there is nothing of any importance that I have to do ...... I can just be ...... I make myself comfortable and let my eyes close naturally ...... shutting out the outside world ...... allowing me to focus fully on the relaxation spreading down my body ...... and I will hear in my mind the numbers counting down from 10 to 1 and with each descending number ...... I will notice relaxation spreading down my body ...... pleasant feelings of deep relaxation ...... warmth and comfort spreading down my body as each muscle just lets go of any unnecessary tension ...... and so as I focus on the sensations in my face as I silently communicate the number 10 ...... as I become aware of the muscles in my forehead letting go ...... the little muscles around my eyes ...... any tension just melting away ...... from my cheeks and around my nose and mouth ...... as the relaxation spreads down into my jaw ...... just letting go ...... 9 ...... as the relaxation spreads down into my neck ...... really letting go ...... 8 as I become aware of the pleasant sensations flowing down into my shoulders ...... as my shoulders sink deeper and deeper ...... letting go ...... as though a weight has been lifted off my shoulders ......

allowing me to fully relax ...... 7 and the warmth travels down both of my arms ...... all the way down ...... into my hands and fingers ...... sweeping down ...... relaxing each and every muscle ...... all the way down ...... as I hear the number 6 and I become aware of the pleasant feelings drifting down my back ...... starting at the top of my spine ...... all the way down my spine ...... each muscle letting go ...... any tension just melting away ...... as my body sinks deeper and deeper into a beautifully relaxed state ...... cascading down ...... 5 as the warmth spreads into my chest and down into my abdomen ...... 4 as I become aware of a wave of relaxation spreading down into my hips ...... and down into my thighs ...... 3 ...... and down past my knees into my lower legs ...... 2 ...... all the muscles just letting go ...... any unnecessary tension drifting away ...... all the way down ...... to 1 ...... as the relaxation spreads into my ankles ...... my feet ...... my toes ...... and the whole of my physical body can just rest and rejuvenate ...... as I can even imagine what it would be like to imagine allowing myself to relax down past 1 to 0 ...... and then even into minus numbers ...... as I wonder what it would be like to imagine how relaxed I would feel at minus 1 ...... or even minus 10 ...... or even minus 100 ...... in fact I realize I can choose to relax all the way down to minus 1,000 ...... as I just allow my mind to drift to a pleasant place ......

MAIN POINTS

▶ Imagine physical relaxation spreading down your body.
▶ Communicate feelings of relaxation spreading down into each part of your body while silently counting down from 10 to minus 1.
▶ Each number from 10 to 1 corresponds to a different part of the body. 10 – head and face, 9 – neck, 8 – shoulders, 7 – arms and hands, 6 – back, 5 – chest and abdomen, 4 – hips, 3 thighs, 2 lower legs, 1 feet and toes.
▶ When reaching 1, imagine drifting down into minus numbers.
▶ Allow your mind to drift to a pleasant place.
▶ Repeat any important phrases to reinforce their meaning.

THINGS TO REMEMBER

▶ Using numbers and counting down are a natural way of focusing attention and producing an altered state. These techniques allow for the state to become conditioned so that every time you use the technique you will find it easier to enter into the altered state of hypnosis.

14

Resume an alert state of consciousness

In this chapter you will learn:
• *how to return to a normal, everyday state after self-hypnosis.*

Before resuming a normal alert state of awareness

The period just prior to resuming a normal waking state is generally considered to be the most conducive to producing specific change. The unconscious mind is very receptive in this state and you can use specific techniques to benefit your psychological and physical well-being. These techniques are described in the subsequent chapters.

Simply spending time in an altered state is beneficial in itself, and you can conclude your self-hypnosis following a short period of allowing your mind to experience a pleasant place. This will encourage the production of positive chemicals in your brain, leading to increased feelings of well-being following hypnosis. When experiencing this pleasant, safe place you can communicate positive feelings of well-being to yourself which encourages more positive thoughts in the waking state. For example, you can state that you will feel full of energy and feel physically fit and healthy. You can personalize the suggestions to suit your needs. You can reinforce positive behaviours, for example, stating 'I will enjoy building my strength and becoming more toned by going to the gym.' My favourite self-communication to use is that I will have all the energy to do all the things I have to do but also all the energy I need to do all the things I want to do. This is similar to using positive affirmations in the normal waking state. The benefit of using positive affirmations in self-hypnosis is that they take effect much more easily as they are processed by the unconscious mind.

Script for positive communications prior to resuming everyday state

I now feel so deeply relaxed ...... so deeply comfortable ...... that my mind ...... is very receptive to what I say ...... and as I am so deeply relaxed and comfortable that everything I say to myself can help me in positive ways in my life ...... as all these thoughts will sink into my unconscious mind ...... the part of me that knows ...... and understands ...... and I will notice positive changes in my life ...... because I am ready for them to happen ...... as each day goes by ...... I will feel physically stronger ...... and fitter in every way ...... I will notice feeling more alert ...... I will feel enthusiastic ...... I will feel motivated to do all the things I have to do ...... I will feel motivated to do all the things I want to do ...... I will focus easily ...... as I feel more optimistic ...... more energetic ...... than I have felt in a long, long while ...... feeling really good about myself ...... feeling really good about the possibilities ...... enjoying being me ......

And I wonder what new things I will choose to do?. ...... as I feel I have all the energy to do all the things I have to do ...... and I have all the energy I need to do all the things I want to do ...... I realize I have time ...... that I can feel calm and relaxed ...... and I will notice that my relationships with other people are easy and pleasurable ...... I am cheerful and content ...... enjoying and looking forward to the opportunities ahead ...... feeling calm ...... feeling strong ...... as I wake up refreshed and alert each morning ...... after a deep refreshing sleep ...... feeling optimistic and cheerful ......

And these feelings of calm will allow me to be creative in my thinking ...... as new possibilities emerge ...... and naturally I will expand my world ...... and develop much more belief in myself ...... and I am now so deeply relaxed ...... and comfortable ...... and just enjoying a time when there is nothing of any importance for me to do ...... I can just be ...... and my mind is so receptive to my inner communications that everything I communicate now ...... in this deeply relaxed state ...... will help me in a positive way in my everyday life ...... and as a result of my inner rest and rejuvenation I will feel healthy and full of vitality ...... I will feel confident and optimistic ...... looking forward to things in life ...... but also enjoying the here and now ...... and these good feelings will grow and develop as my level of confidence increases and I feel really good about myself ...... really enjoying being me ...... when I do resume my normal everyday waking state I will notice that I feel good and have all the energy I need to do all the things I have to do but also all the energy I need to do all the things I want to do ...... as I notice more positive things in life ...... and I will feel confident and optimistic ...... relaxed and calm ......

MAIN POINTS

▶ Before you resume a normal waking state give yourself some positive suggestions of well-being.
▶ You can tailor these suggestion so that they are specific to you.
▶ Make positive suggestions, such as feeling cheerful and optimistic.

Resuming a normal alert state of consciousness

Resuming a normal level of alert awareness brings your period of self-hypnosis to an end. The process involves allowing your brain to return to a more alert state in which the cortex increases its activity and makes you fully conscious and aware. While in hypnosis you have been in a state of internal focus. To end your state of self-hypnosis you adjust this awareness to focus externally once again.

Top tip
When resuming a normal waking state, always say the words *'every part of me is back here in the present'*. This is a key phrase that you can use to allow yourself to become fully alert and awake. Using this phrase ensures that any processing is completed and your brain can resume a normal state of processing.

Your inner voice should be louder and more rapid than when you were giving yourself suggestions for relaxation. You do not need to leave pauses. Start off slowly and as you become more and more awake you will find your inner voice will naturally be more conscious and alert.

It may take a few moments for you to become fully alert. You may find that when you have opened your eyes, your body still feels quite heavy and lethargic. Have a stretch and you will soon feel alert again. It is quite normal to feel a bit 'spaced out' when you first open your eyes. You may not have been aware of how relaxed you were until you return to an alert state. In fact, within a few minutes this feeling of sleepiness will be replaced by feeling more alert, and often people experience a surge of energy and a feeling of rejuvenation following self-hypnosis.

Script for re-establishing an everyday state

When I am ready ...... and only then ...... and when my unconscious mind has finished any processing ...... I will naturally return to a normal alert level of consciousness ...... I will become aware of my physical body ...... as I notice becoming aware of the sounds around me ...... aware of every part of me being awake ...... and aware of the things around me ...... just as soon as I am ready my eyes will gently open and I will be aware that *every part of me is back here in the present* ...... I am once again becoming aware of where I am ...... I am aware of the outside world around me ...... I am aware of feeling great ...... refreshed ...... rejuvenated ...... and so I will just allow my eyes to open as soon as I am ready ...... just allow my eyes to open ...... gently in my own time ...... feeling refreshed ...... rejuvenated ...... relaxed and calm ...... looking forward ...... feeling positive and full of energy.

MAIN POINTS

▶ Change you focus of awareness back to reality.
▶ Become aware of your body.
▶ Become aware of where you are.
▶ State 'every part of me is back here in the present'.
▶ Open your eyes.
▶ Have a stretch and reinforce feelings of alertness and well-being.

THINGS TO REMEMBER

▶ Prior to ending your period of self-hypnosis there is an ideal opportunity for you to communicate to yourself positive feelings of well-being. This will encourage these positive experiences in your everyday life. When you choose to end your time in self-hypnosis you can return to a normal alert state by focusing your awareness externally. Always say the words *'every part of me is back here in the present'* to ensure that your unconscious mind has completed any internal processing.

Part 4

How to use self-hypnosis for a better life – psychological well-being

15

How to increase psychological well-being

In this chapter you will learn:
• *what influences psychological well-being.*

Specific psychological techniques can be used within self-hypnosis to enhance psychological well-being. Psychology, the scientific study of mind and behaviour, has traditionally focused on alleviating psychological distress. The past 20 years have seen a change of focus with the emergence of Positive Psychology. Positive Psychology is the science of positive aspects of human life, such as happiness and well-being, specifically, how creating positive well-being can enrich and enhance people's lives and communities. It is not targeted at alleviating mental health problems, but is focused on researching and developing techniques to increase psychological well-being. Psychological well-being refers to how we feel about ourselves and our capacity to live a full and productive life. It also refers to individuals having the flexibility to deal with life's inevitable challenges. It includes such things as self-acceptance, optimism, motivation, creativity and confidence. Research shows that individuals with positive psychological well-being are happier, feel more satisfied with their lives, are more productive and have better relationships.

The important findings from psychology in the last few years show that psychological well-being can be learned. Only about 50% of well-being or happiness is determined by genes. Research indicates a further 15% is determined by standard of living and social interactions. The remaining 35% can be influenced by thinking and behaviour. Hypnosis offers an effective way of helping you to influence your thoughts and behaviour positively.

Experiencing positive emotions during self-hypnosis makes the generation of positive emotions more likely to occur in everyday life. They also have the added benefit of helping people cope better with negative experiences. Research shows that the generation of positive emotions makes negative emotions dissipate more readily. Individuals who experience positive emotions are more likely to find meaning in negative events, and this in turn leads to an increase in positive emotions. In other words positive emotions act as a buffer against negative experiences. They are a coping mechanism and make your more resilient.

Psychological well-being can be influenced in two ways: first by engaging in specific techniques designed to increase well-being and second, by learning to develop coping mechanisms to help reduce the negative impact of life's inevitable difficulties. Self-hypnosis is a particularly useful psychological technique to enable you to cope with negative stressors and increase positive mood and well-being, through increasing positivity, increasing motivation, increasing optimism, enhancing creativity and developing self-acceptance.

THINGS TO REMEMBER

▶ Positive psychology is the study of positive aspects of human life and psychological well-being. Techniques to increase well-being and increase positive emotions can be used within self-hypnosis.

16

Positivity

In this chapter you will learn:
- *a script for experiencing a positive state of mind*
- *a script for experiencing gratefulness.*

Positive states of mind

Hypnosis is particularly beneficial for producing positive states of mind as it involves engaging parts of the brain that regulate emotion. The mind and body are intrinsically linked and the body produces physical and mental responses to emotions. During self-hypnosis you can condition your body and mind to experience positive well-being more frequently in your everyday life. In the following technique you use the natural communications systems of the body to create positive well-being. When an individual feels an emotion, such as joy, there is an accompanying physical sensation. There has been a long debate in psychology concerning which comes first, the physical sensation or the recognition of the emotion. Recent evidence suggests that they both play a role and influence each other. Experiencing a pleasant physical sensation in the body sends messages to the brain that it can produce happy chemicals which produce joyful thoughts. This feedback mechanism is useful in hypnosis as you can create a positive mindset by imagining the physical sensation that you experience when feeling happy and joyful. Your brain creates memories of the positive state regardless of whether it is imaginary or real. Creating these experiences during self-hypnosis makes them more likely to occur in your everyday life. You can use any technique of your choice to enter hypnosis. Included here is a generic relaxation technique but you can vary this according to your requirement and preferences.

Script for experiencing a positive state of mind

As I gently close my eyes and focus on my breathing, in ...... and out ...... and while I continue to focus on my breathing I realize there is nothing of importance for me to do ...... just to be ...... this is my time ...... a time just for me ...... a time for me to really concentrate on myself ...... I am just going to let myself focus on my favourite place in nature ...... and it's a beautiful day ...... I notice the sky is a special shade of blue, very clear ...... it's a warm day ...... a warm summer's day ...... there is a dazzling sun in the sky ...... and ...... it's so bright that I just want to relax and enjoying feeling the warmth of the sun on my body ...... and surprisingly I find that I can direct the sun's rays over my body, and as I realize this, I begin to direct the light from the sun over my face ...... I can see its light as a golden stream of bright yellow and orange ...... and I can feel the warmth of the light from the sun on my face ...... just relaxing those muscles across my forehead ...... drifting down around the eyes and the nose and mouth ...... and as I do this ...... I find that the facial muscles begin to flatten out as they relax ...... and I let go ...... all the way ...... as the warmth spreads down into my jaw ...... letting go of any tension ......

And it's a beautiful day ...... I move the light from the sun on to my neck ...... feeling the warmth of the sun over my neck, relaxing all those muscles, letting go ...... as the sunlight moves down across my shoulders I feel my shoulders letting go of any tension ...... like a weight has been lifted off them ...... realize how relaxed I feel ...... so comfortable and at peace with the world ...... all of my focused attention on the warm feelings of relaxation spreading down through my body ...... and as I direct the light from the sun down my right arm ...... seeing ...... feeling the warmth of the sun ...... the glow from the orange beam of light ...... down from the shoulders to the tips of the fingers ...... the right arm begins to relax and let go ...... relax and let go ...... and it's a beautiful feeling to be here right now ...... the warmth of the light from the sun penetrates the nerves and bones and muscles of that right arm all the way through ...... it is such a beautiful day ...... as I move the sun over to my left arm and guide the light from the sun down the left arm ...... from the top of the shoulders all the way down to the tips of the fingers ...... I can feel the left arm relaxing ......

becoming heavy ...... and comfortable and relaxed ...... now the light moves across and into the chest area and the chest and all the muscles there relax ...... my breathing deepens quite naturally ...... slow deep breathing ...... without effort ...... and the relaxation continues down into my abdomen ...... and all the way down to my hips and thighs and over to the right leg ...... the beautiful warmth of the sun sinks all the way down the leg ...... relaxing every muscle ...... down to my toes ...... all the way down the left leg from the top of the hips all the way down to the tips of my toes ...... I just let go of any tension ...... and it's a beautiful day ...... I am now only aware of how my body feels ...... totally and completely relaxed ...... from the top of my head to the tips of my toes ...... and as I become less aware of my body ...... I realize that I can just forget my physical body ...... as I notice that I am not fully aware of all of my body ...... as it rests so peacefully ...... and I can just forget about it ...... and I can just rest here and as my mind relaxes even further I just notice the sun in the sky going down as the day comes to an end ...... with the sun going down ...... further down in the sky ...... deeper and deeper ...... and the sky is ablaze with an abundance of colours of crimson and bright purple and blue and yellow streaks ...... and it's a beautiful evening ...... and the sun goes further and further down ...... over the horizon, until ...... all that is left ...... is a black ...... velvety sky ...... and twinkling up there in the sky is a single shining star ...... and I find myself completely engrossed in that one star ...... nothing else matters except this beautiful single solitary sparkling star in the sky ...... and it's a beautiful night ...... apart from the one star it is very dark, but I feel so safe ...... so comfortable ...... so relaxed ...... and calm ...... as I find myself moving towards that star in the sky ...... moving up ...... and up and up ...... my body feels weightless as it lifts up to the star ...... going higher and higher, up and up ...... and as the star grows bigger and bigger I realize I am getting quite close to the star ...... closer to its beauty and light ...... as it just gets bigger and bigger ...... brighter and brighter ...... until all at once I am that star in the night sky ...... that beautiful star ...... twinkling away ...... that silver solitary star in the night sky ...... I become the star and the star is me ...... and it's a beautiful star ...... and I find myself drifting deeper and deeper ...... becoming even more deeply relaxed ...... just letting go ...... deeper and deeper ...... into an inner peace ...... as I allow my mind to drift to a special place of comfort ...... as I imagine my perfect place ...... my special place ...... a pleasant place ...... where I can just be ......

And now I am so deeply relaxed and comfortable ...... and I am aware that I may not even be aware of my physical body resting so comfortably ...... and as I experience a sense of drifting ...... in both my mind and my body ...... as I realize that the usual limitations in my thinking are no longer applicable ...... as I have access to my unconscious mind ...... the part of my mind that is so receptive to new learning ...... I wonder at the vast resources held in my unconscious mind ...... all the positive things I've ever experienced are lodged somewhere in my unconscious mind ...... happy memories I may not have thought of for a very long time ...... and my body can remember what it feels like to feel joy ...... and can imagine what it feels like to feel immense joy ...... overwhelming joy and happiness ...... not about anything ...... just pure joy ...... I begin to focus on a warm feeling developing within my body ...... a bright feeling ...... maybe starting in the middle of my body ...... building up inside me ...... as if its coming from deep inside me ...... as I enjoy allowing this feeling to fully develop ...... as it develops into a bright cheerful colour ...... I can just feel these sensations bubbling up within me ...... sending energy all through my body ...... and I begin to notice my whole body feels lighter ...... brighter ...... I can just let my mind enjoy ...... feeling this good ...... and I may even remember happy memories ...... and I can just enjoy feeling great ...... excited ...... joyful ...... and I can even allow myself to develop these positive feelings even more ...... imagining what it would be like to feel even more positive ...... alive ...... and well ...... having all the energy I need to do all the things I have to do ...... feeling happy ...... and I see myself smiling ...... and the warm feelings continue to develop within me ...... brighter and lighter ...... as I realize it is quite natural to feel this good ...... relaxed and yet full of vibrant energy ...... cascading through my body ...... and I realize that I can feel this good naturally and easily ...... and I will notice in my everyday life ...... good feelings ...... feeling happy ...... feeling enthusiastic ...... and feeling positive ...... as I realize the positive physical sensations in my body feel so good ...... and I will notice these positive feelings more often in my everyday life ...... as my body naturally generates positive feelings ...... and with these feelings ...... come positive emotions ...... allowing me to enjoy feeling confident and optimistic ...... and these good feelings and positive thoughts will occur much more frequently ...... because I realize how good it feels to feel this good ...... and as my whole body fills with this cheerful colour ...... this feeling of vitality ...... I feel a sense of pleasure within me ...... cascading good feelings all through my body ......

...... as I am now so deeply relaxed and comfortable ...... and just enjoying a time when there is nothing of any importance for me to do ...... I can just be ...... and my mind is so receptive to my inner communications that everything I communicate now ...... in this deeply relaxed state ...... will help me in a positive way in my everyday life ...... and as a result of my inner rest and rejuvenation I will feel healthy and full of vitality ...... I will feel confident and optimistic ...... looking forward to things in life ...... but also enjoying the here and now ...... and these good feelings will grow and develop as my levels of confidence increase and I feel really good about myself ...... really enjoying being me ...... when I do resume my normal everyday waking state I will notice that I feel good and have all the energy I need to do all the things I have to do, but also all the energy I need to do all the things I want to do ...... as I notice more positive things in life ...... I will feel confident and optimistic ...... relaxed and calm ......

As only as soon as I am ready ...... and my unconscious mind has finished any processing ...... I will naturally return to a normal alert level of consciousness ...... I will become aware of my physical body ...... as I notice becoming aware of the sounds around me ...... aware of every part of me being awake ...... I am once again becoming aware of where I am ...... and the things around me ...... just as soon as I am ready my eyes will gently open and *every part of me is back here in the present* ...... I am aware of the outside world around me ...... I am aware of feeling great ...... refreshed ...... rejuvenated ...... and so I will just allow my eyes to open as soon as I am ready ...... to just allow my eyes to open ...... gently in my own time ...... feeling refreshed ...... rejuvenated ...... relaxed and calm ...... looking forward ...... feeling positive and full of energy ......

MAIN POINTS

▶ Once you have achieved an altered state of hypnosis focus on the feeling of joy within your body.

▶ Allow yourself to experience the warm, positive feelings that develop in your body.

▶ Develop these sensations by imagining a vibrant, cheerful colour developing within your body.

- ▶ Send this colourful energy all round your body.
- ▶ Communicate positive suggestions.
- ▶ Return to a normal alert state.

Gratefulness

Gratitude, or thankfulness, and well-being are connected. The more grateful you are the happier you are – scientific evidence provides support for this. There is also evidence that gratefulness can be increased and that increasing feelings of gratefulness leads to increased well-being. When positive thoughts are plentiful then your brain is awash with positive chemicals. Encouraging the brain to produce positive chemicals while in a state of hypnosis has long-term positive benefits. It can increase mood in the normal waking state. Thoughts become habitual. The generation of positive thoughts when in a state of hypnosis leads to a greater likelihood of positive thoughts in the normal waking state. Research shows that one of the best ways of encouraging positive thoughts and to encourage positive brain processes is to consider what one is grateful for. This is one technique used in Positive Psychology that can be used within self-hypnosis with great effect. Studies have shown us that increasing gratitude can enhance positive memory recall in normal everyday life. The great Roman orator Cicero wrote, 'Gratitude is not only the greatest of virtues, but the parent of all the others.' This acknowledges the wide-reaching positive effects thankfulness can create. There is a wealth of scientific evidence showing positive benefits of increasing gratefulness. Gratefulness and relaxation are symbiotic. In other words, when one feels thankful for something there is a corresponding increase of physical relaxation. When deeply relaxed, the mind is highly receptive to positive thoughts. This relationship promotes the positive benefits.

Top tip

When in a deep state of self-hypnosis, and prior to concluding your state of self-hypnosis, allow your mind to consider three things that you are grateful for in your life. It may be that you appreciate small things, like having a warm bed to sleep in, or that you are grateful it's the weekend soon and you can sleep in. You may find that you wish to consider more fundamental aspects of life, such as freedom or good health. It is often useful to think of people who have helped you or enriched your life in some way, large or small. Allow yourself to consider all the aspects that make you grateful. Explore what it means to you. Enjoy those positive feelings. You may find your mind recalling things from the past that you are thankful for. That is fine.

Script for gratefulness task

As I enjoy allowing myself some time …… just to relax …… and so knowing there is nothing of any importance that I have to do …… I can just be …… as I make myself comfortable and let my eyes close naturally …… shutting out the outside world …… allowing me to fully focus on the relaxation spreading down my body …… and I will hear in my mind the numbers counting down from 10 to 1 and with each descending number …… I will notice relaxation spreading down my body …… pleasant feelings of deep relaxation …… warmth and comfort spread down my body as each muscle just lets go of any unnecessary tension …… and so as I focus on the sensations in my face as I silently communicate the number 10 …… as I become aware of the muscles in my forehead letting go …… the little muscles around my eyes …… any tension just melting away …… into my cheeks and around my nose and mouth …… as the relaxation spreads down into my jaw …… just letting go …… 9 …… as the relaxation spreads down into my neck …… really letting go …… 8 as I become aware of the pleasant sensations flowing down into my shoulders …… as my shoulders sink deeper and deeper …… letting go …… as though a weight has been lifted off my shoulders …… allowing me to fully relax …… 7 and the warmth travels down both of my arms …… all the way down …… into my hands and fingers …… sweeping down …… relaxing each and every muscle …… all the way down …… as I hear the number 6 and I become aware of the pleasant feelings drifting down my back …… starting at the top of my spine …… all the way down my spine …… each muscle letting go …… any tension just melting away …… as my body sinks deeper and deeper into a beautifully relaxed state …… cascading down …… 5 as the warmth spreads into my chest and down into my abdomen …… 4 as I become aware of a wave of relaxation spreading down into my hips ...... and down into my thighs ...... 3 ...... and down past my knees into my lower legs ...... 2 ...... all the muscles just letting go ...... any unnecessary tension drifting away ...... all the way down ...... to 1 ...... as the relaxation spreads into my ankles ...... my feet ...... my toes ...... and the whole of my physical body can just rest and rejuvenate ...... as I can even imagine what it would be like to imagine allowing myself to relax down past 1 to 0 ...... and then even into minus numbers ...... as I wonder what it would be like to imagine how relaxed I feel at minus 1 ...... or even minus 10 ...... or even minus 100 ...... in fact I realize I can just choose to relax all the way down to minus 1,000 ...... as I just allow my mind to drift to a pleasant place ......

...... and in this beautifully relaxed state it is easy to allow my mind to consider the things that I am grateful for ...... things in my life that make me feel really thankful ...... as I consider now something that I am grateful for ...... and I consider what makes me feel so thankful ...... and how pleasant is it to appreciate ...... to acknowledge to myself that I feel grateful ......

(give yourself some time to really examine and enjoy the thing that you have chosen)

...... and now my mind can drift to consider another thing that I am grateful for ...... and how good that makes me feel ...... as I fully appreciate whatever I am thankful for ...... and my mind can easily access more things in my life that I feel grateful for ...... and I can just let these good feelings of gratefulness wash over me ...... as I ponder on how beneficial it is to take time to stop and appreciate ...... all that I am grateful for ...... and I let these good feelings enrich me ...... as I give heart-felt thanks ...... for all the things I am thankful for ......

...... and I am now so deeply relaxed ...... and comfortable ...... and just enjoying a time when there is nothing of any importance for me to do ...... I can just be ...... and my mind is so receptive to my inner communications that everything I communicate now ...... in this deeply relaxed state ...... will help me in a positive way in my everyday life ...... and as a result of my inner rest and rejuvenation I will feel healthy and full of vitality ...... I will feel confident and optimistic ...... looking forward to things in life ...... but also enjoying the here and now ...... and these good feelings will grow and develop as my levels of confidence increase and I feel really good about myself ...... really enjoying being me ...... when I do resume my normal everyday waking state I will feel notice that I feel good and have all the energy I need to do all the things I have to do but also all the energy I need to do all the things I want to do ...... as I notice more positive things in life ...... and I will feel confident and optimistic ...... relaxed and calm ......

Only as soon as I am ready ...... and my unconscious mind has finished any processing ...... I will naturally return to a normal alert level of consciousness ...... I will become aware of my physical body ...... as I notice becoming aware of the sounds around me ...... aware of every part of me being awake ...... I am once again becoming aware of where I am ...... and the things around me ...... just as soon as I am ready my eyes will gently open and *every part of me is back here in the present* ...... I am aware of the outside world around me ...... I am aware of feeling great ...... refreshed ...... rejuvenated ...... and so I will just allow my eyes to open as soon as I am ready ...... to just allow my eyes to open ...... gently in my own time ...... feeling refreshed ...... rejuvenated ...... relaxed and calm ...... looking forward ...... feeling positive and full of energy ......

MAIN POINTS

▶ When in a deep state of self-hypnosis consider three things that you are thankful for in life.
▶ Consider all the aspects of the thing or person that you feel grateful about.
▶ Fully appreciate all that you are thankful for.
▶ Communicate positive suggestions.
▶ Return to a normal alert state.

THINGS TO REMEMBER

▶ Positive Psychology research offers a wealth of scientific evidence that encouraging positive states of mind, and in particular increasing gratefulness, leads to positive well-being. Using these techniques with self-hypnosis can magnify their effects and lead to greater positive well-being and increased happiness in your everyday life.

17

Motivation

In this chapter you will learn:
- *techniques to increase your motivation and sense of purpose in life.*

Motivation and having a purpose in life have been shown to be highly influential on happiness and psychological well-being. A lack of motivation is a common complaint. As humans, motivation is crucial and we are designed to seek reward. The brain is designed to reinforce positive behaviour. The brain produces a chemical called dopamine in response to certain behaviours. This natural reward system of the brain ensures survival. The aspects of life that are crucial to survival are the most reinforced through the production of dopamine, for example, eating, drinking and reproducing. Other behaviours in life are also reinforced through the production of dopamine. If behaviour is rewarding you feel more motivated to do it, through the production of dopamine. The production of dopamine results in wanting to engage in that behaviour again. Many aspects of psychological well-being are influenced by motivation.

In life motivation is crucial. Without it we would not survive. We need motivation to work, to provide for ourselves and others, to engage in leisure activities, to engage in relationships with others, and to lead full and productive lives. High levels of motivation are also fundamental to achieving extraordinary things in life, such as excelling at sport, whether professionally or as a hobby, or achieving great things at work or at home.

> **Insight**
> Feeling motivated feels good. It is a positive state of mind.

There are two main facets to motivating activities; wanting and enjoying. The reward for getting something you want and the enjoyment from liking what you get. The 'wanting' is produced by dopamine; the 'liking' is caused by an increase in another chemical, serotonin. These two chemicals interact. Dopamine is heavily involved in goal-directed behaviour and therefore is crucial to motivation and leading a productive and satisfying life. If the brain does not produce sufficient dopamine the effects are lethargy, lack of motivation and lack of drive. This can in turn affect the levels of serotonin and low mood can occur.

Motivation, and therefore dopamine levels, can be increased through changing behaviour, thoughts and beliefs. Motivation is based on intrinsic and extrinsic reward. Intrinsic reward refers to internal feelings, feeling good and gaining pleasure. Extrinsic reward refers to external motivators such as earning money, gaining accolades and outward success. Research has shown that over-reliance on external motivators can result in less intrinsic motivation. This can reduce pleasure and ultimately reduce motivation. Achieving high intrinsic motivation is important to positive psychological well-being. Intrinsic motivation is dependent on thoughts and beliefs.

How to increase motivation

Imagery has long been used in hypnosis as a method of increasing motivation. The parts of the brain that become active when carrying out an activity are also activated when you imagine the behaviour. During hypnosis the part of the brain that governs our ability to imagine what an experience will be like, the insula, is more active. This allows the imagination to have a stronger effect and you can develop memory traces of the imagined experience. Imagining behaviour makes that behaviour more likely to occur because the brain has already experienced it. Self-hypnosis also allows you to change your perception. Believing you can achieve something allows you to see the possibilities in a more positive way. This change in thought processes allows your mind to perceive the activity as more attainable. This leads to an increase in motivation and makes you more likely to achieve your goals.

Imagery technique to use with self-hypnosis

When you are comfortable in a pleasant, deep state of self-hypnosis allow yourself to fantasize about what you really want. Like daydreaming, create in your mind the experience you would like to achieve. Make the experience as vivid as possible. Imagine sounds and colours, smells and textures.

In your imagination focus on attaining the thing you desire rather than the process of achieving it. Imagine your desired reality. Allow yourself to really enjoy the experience of achieving your goal, whether it is getting a new job, being confident in meetings, mastering a hobby or winning a race. During self-hypnosis there is freedom from worry about failure as the conscious critical parts of your mind are less active. This allows you to experience attaining your goal without questioning, and results in the increase of positive brain chemicals which reinforce the good feelings and help cement positive beliefs that you can achieve your goal. These positive thoughts encourage motivation as they affect the levels of dopamine and serotonin in the brain.

Using your imagination within self-hypnosis to create experiences allows 'flow' to develop. 'Flow' is the mental state in which a person is fully immersed in an activity. It is a single-minded immersion. You may experience 'flow' in your everyday life when you are engaged in motivating activities. In flow the emotions are channelled, positive and energized. Conducting this process in self-hypnosis allows the unconscious part of your mind to be fully engaged with the process of attainment and you may be surprised at new and original ideas emerging either during the hypnosis state or in the forthcoming hours and days. You may think of new possibilities or be able to see answers to problems you hadn't thought of before. This is due to your unconscious mind processing the information and then thoughts emerging into consciousness.

It may be useful to keep a notepad and pen nearby so that when you finish your session of self-hypnosis you can note down any interesting ideas and experiences you have in self-hypnosis.

Script for creating the environment of motivation

As I focus on my breathing ...... in and out ...... just slowing down with each breath ...... and I can just lie (or sit) here ...... enjoying a bit of time for me ...... some space for me ...... just to relax ...... and I can allow my imagination to drift ...... as I imagine I am standing at the top of a beautiful staircase ...... and I can imagine the stairs in front of me ...... stretching down ...... I can feel the banister as my hand rests upon it ...... and I feel safe and secure ...... standing at the top of this staircase ...... and my mind imagines where the staircase is taking me to ...... to a place where I feel safe and comfortable ...... relaxed ...... into my own inner world ...... where I feel completely comfortable ...... and in a moment I am going to walk down the stairs, one step at a time ...... and with each step down the stairs ...... I will notice that I feel more and more relaxed ...... allowing myself to go deeper and deeper into a beautiful state of deep relaxation and hypnosis ...... I will begin to count down from 10 to 1 and with each descending number I will take one step down the stairs ...... with each descending number I will find myself becoming one tenth or ten per cent even more absorbed ...... with each descending number and each step down the stairs I will feel more and more deeply relaxed ...... (*begin counting down slowly and silently from 10 to 1 and imagine yourself walking down the stairs, one step at a time*) 10 ...... 9 ...... and with each step down I allow myself to drift deeper ...... 8 ...... deeper and deeper ...... 7 ...... as very pleasant sensations of safety and comfort spread down through my body ...... 6 ...... with every breath just letting go ...... 5 ...... deeper and deeper still ...... 4 ...... and I notice as I go down the stairs how detached I feel ...... entering into my own world ...... 3 ...... 2 ...... all the way down into my special place ...... a place just for me ...... where I feel safe and secure ...... happy and relaxed ...... all the way down ...... deeper and deeper ...... 1 ...... and as I reach the bottom step ...... and step off I can continue to allow myself to drift even deeper ......

as deeply as I choose to go ...... all the way ...... as deep as I choose ...... (*pause here and just allow yourself to be – experience whatever occurs*) and I can allow myself to drift just as deeply as I wish ...... imagining what it would be like to go down past 1 ...... down to 0 ...... and even down into minus numbers ...... all the way ...... down to minus 1 ...... minus 5 ...... minus 10 ...... even down to minus 50 ...... minus 100 ...... as my mind can take me on a special journey wherever it wants me to go ...... to a special place ...... all the way ...... deeper and deeper ...... to a pleasant place ......

As I am now so deeply relaxed and comfortable ...... and my mind is so receptive to new ideas and fresh ways of looking at things in my life ...... I can become fully aware of feeling physically relaxed and mentally calm ...... as I naturally generate positive feelings of well-being ...... as I become even more comfortable ...... I can take a break ...... and allow my imagination to take me on a journey ...... a journey using my unconscious mind ...... the part of me that allows me to perform in the best way I can ...... the part of me with ample resources that I can access ...... helping me to be the person I wish to be ...... and so I can use my imagination to create the experience of achieving whatever I want to achieve ...... and I don't even need to worry about the process ...... as I know I have the internal resources to motivate myself to achieve ...... whatever I choose ...... as I notice feeling happy and calm ...... relaxed ...... and yet excited about the possibilities ahead ...... the mental picture becomes clearer and clearer ...... I can even begin to see details ...... as I can see myself there ...... as I notice the clothes I am wearing ...... and I can just relax and watch myself ...... I become aware of how positive and confident I appear ...... as I can just watch myself achieving ...... partaking ...... enjoying ...... (*allow your unconscious mind to create a dream like experience imagining yourself achieving your goal*) ...... and I find myself becoming so aware of what I want to achieve and ...... why I want to achieve ...... that I now realize that I can achieve whatever I want to achieve ...... as there are so few limitations ...... and as I watch myself and experience the joy of achieving my goal ...... knowing that I can allow my internal resources to help me achieve that goal ...... enjoying having achieved it ...... and let these good feelings cascade through my body ...... giving me energy ...... vitality ...... strength ...... and the new learnings I have made will allow me to achieve in my everyday life ...... as I realize what I need to do ...... what I can do ...... without the usual limitations ...... that I no longer need ......

...... and I am now so deeply relaxed ...... and comfortable ...... and just enjoying a time when there is nothing of any importance for me to do ...... I can just be ...... and my mind is so receptive to my inner communications that everything I communicate now ...... in this deeply relaxed state ...... will help me in a positive way in my everyday life ...... and as a result of my inner rest and rejuvenation I will feel healthy and full of vitality ...... I will feel confident and optimistic ...... looking forward to things in life ...... but also enjoying the here and now ...... and these good feelings will grow and develop as my levels of confidence increase and I feel really good about myself ...... really enjoying being me ...... when I do resume my normal everyday waking state I will notice that I feel good and have all the energy I need to do all the things I have to do but also all the energy I need to do all the things I want to do ...... as I notice more positive things in life ...... and I will feel confident and optimistic ...... relaxed and calm ......

Only as soon as I am ready ...... and my unconscious mind has finished any processing ...... I will naturally return to a normal alert level of consciousness ...... I will become aware of my physical body ...... as I notice becoming aware of the sounds around me ...... aware of every part of me being awake ...... I am once again becoming aware of where I am ...... and the things around me ...... just as soon as I am ready my eyes will gently open and *every part of me is back here in the present* ...... I am aware of the outside world around me ...... I am aware of feeling great ...... refreshed ...... rejuvenated ...... and so I will just allow my eyes to open as soon as I am ready ...... to just allow my eyes to open ...... gently in my own time ...... feeling refreshed ...... rejuvenated ...... relaxed and calm ...... looking forward ...... feeling positive and full of energy ......

MAIN POINTS

▶ Once you have achieved an altered state of hypnosis focus on whatever you want to achieve.
▶ Create the experience of actually attaining what you want.
▶ Do not focus on the process. Focus on the outcome.
▶ Enjoy the good feelings associated with achieving your goal.
▶ Communicate positive suggestions.
▶ Return to a normal alert state.

THINGS TO REMEMBER

▶ Motivation plays a key role in positive well-being. Motivation can be increased through techniques in self-hypnosis which allow you to bypass limiting thoughts and beliefs. This can improve your levels of motivation in your everyday life and lead to increased positive well-being.

18

Optimism

In this chapter you will learn:
- *techniques to help you improve your optimism and positivity.*

Optimism, defined as hopefulness and confidence about the future, has an important role to play in psychological well-being. Optimism is closely linked to motivation as optimistic people tend to be much more motivated. 'A pessimist sees the difficulty in every opportunity; an optimist sees the opportunity in every difficulty' said Winston Churchill.

We tend to think of optimism as being a personality trait. Research shows that only about 50% of personality is inherited. So whether you have an optimistic or pessimistic outlook on life is in some ways determined by your genetics. However, personality traits are not set in stone. They are flexible and can develop and grow through life experiences. Optimism is something that can be developed. Specific techniques to use within self-hypnosis have been developed to allow you to produce more optimistic thought patterns.

Insight

Negative thinking creates negativity. Humans naturally try and explain events and particularly other people's thoughts and behaviours. If you think negatively you are likely to interpret other people's actions as negative. This is so unhelpful in life.

People who have an optimistic outlook on life are happier, healthier and more successful. This has been shown over and over again in Positive Psychology research. Optimism has an important role to play in psychological well-being because it enables individuals to cope with negative life events in a more positive way.

An individual with high levels of optimism will react to a negative life event in ways that will protect their well-being. Negative events are seen as:

▶ temporary setbacks
▶ isolated to particular circumstances
▶ something that can be overcome by effort and abilities.

Perceiving negative events in this way allows you to feel in control and able to cope with the situation. Adequate coping mechanisms protect you from negative events and you can maintain high levels of motivation and confidence even in times of difficulty.

Someone with low levels of optimism will react to a negative life event with beliefs that can lead to feelings of helplessness. This can lead to a reduction in psychological well-being. Negative life events are seen as:

▶ lasting a long time
▶ negatively effecting everything
▶ the fault of the individual.

Increasing levels of optimism is beneficial to psychological well-being. Self-hypnosis is an excellent tool to accompany the theoretical knowledge we have learned from examining positive aspects of personality and behaviour. Research has shown that optimism is something that can be increased through using specific techniques. These techniques can be even more powerful if used within self-hypnosis as the brain and mind are more flexible in this state and change can occur quickly.

Increasing optimism and positivity with self-hypnosis

Levels of optimism can be increased to produce positive psychological well-being. One of the ways we can affect optimism is through developing positive thought processes. It is not so much 'what' happens to individuals in life but 'how' individuals 'think' about situations that affect their level of well-being. Thoughts, beliefs and perceptions are important.

Positive thoughts allow for outward thinking. This prevents inward looking habits of self-generated negative thoughts. Negative thinking patterns tend to narrow an individual's thought repertoire and people tend to look inwards, become self-obsessed and think about themselves more than anything else. Thoughts grow in strength the more attention is paid to them. Changing thinking patterns through self-hypnosis can lead to more optimistic thought patterns and result in increased positive well-being.

Humans are biologically driven to explain events, experiences and behaviours. These explanations are called attributions. How we explain experiences affects how we feel about them. It doesn't matter how many positive things occur to a person, if they don't think of them as positive they will not lead to increased happiness or well-being. Having a positive attributional style contributes to levels of optimism and increased motivation as it allows individuals to feel they are in control of their own experiences.

Basic beliefs about ourselves and the world around us form the basis of our well-being. Often beliefs about ourselves, our abilities and our purpose are dictated by our attributional style. Attribution refers to how individuals explain causes of events, other's behaviour, and their own behaviour. Attribution can be internal or external. When an internal attribution is made, the individual sees themselves as causing the event. When an external attribution is made, the cause is seen as due to the situation not the person. How you perceive the cause of positive and negative events in life in part determines your level of optimism and affects your psychological well-being.

Optimistic attributional style

If a person has an optimistic attributional style they tend to see themselves as contributing to positive events but not over-blaming themselves for negative events. A pessimistic attributional style results in the person blaming themselves for bad things and not taking any credit for good events.

Event	Internally attribute cause	Externally attribute cause
Success	Optimistic	Pessimistic
Failure	Pessimistic	Optimistic

Figure 18.1 Optimistic/pessimistic attributional style.

Positive attribution of events is important to psychological well-being because it can lead to greater confidence and self-esteem which in turn leads to more positive psychological well-being. Research has shown that those who have developed optimism:

- ▶ show better academic performance
- ▶ are more productive at work and in social pursuits
- ▶ have greater satisfaction in interpersonal relationships
- ▶ are more effective at coping with life stressors
- ▶ show less vulnerability to depression
- ▶ have superior physical health
- ▶ are happier.

Challenging negative thoughts

Warning

These techniques are designed to help enhance psychological well-being and are not to be used with severe anxiety or any mental health disorder. Always consult your doctor if you have any concerns.

One of the best ways of changing your natural attributional style so that it is more positive and therefore more useful to you is through challenging negative thinking patterns and beliefs.

This technique is based on psychological research which shows that questioning and challenging negative beliefs is useful in creating more positive states. Negative thoughts are continually reinforced in the conscious mind every time we think of them. Thinking about worries or concerns or negative beliefs about ourselves makes them more likely to occur. This can lead to a vicious circle of negative thinking affecting behaviour. For example, a belief that you are shy and lack confidence can be reinforced by your behaviour. You may refrain from social engagements because you believe you will not enjoy them. This only leads to reinforcing your belief because you do not have the opportunity to challenge it.

Insight

Challenging negative thinking, especially in a state of self-hypnosis, where your mind is open to more creative ways of thinking, can help you develop more positive thinking.

During self-hypnosis allow your conscious mind to become aware of any negative thoughts you may have and then ask yourself the following questions:

▶ What is it I believe to be true?
▶ Can I be 100% sure that it is true?
▶ How do I feel if I believe it to be true?
▶ How do I feel if I don't believe it is true?

Following each question allow your unconscious mind an opportunity to process the information. This may take some time. This process allows your unconscious mind to be involved in the conscious questioning and allows you to use the most creative regions of your mind to come up with new and more appropriate thinking. In the conscious waking state we rarely question whether our beliefs are true. We just accept them. In reality, things are rarely as straightforward as they first appear and they may not be true at all. I have paired this technique with a sensory technique as this creates an ideal state for helping you see things from a different perspective when reprocessing thoughts and beliefs.

Script for challenging negative thinking

As I make myself comfortable and rest my eyes ...... I focus on the feelings in my body and just allow myself to let go of any tension

...... my breathing naturally deepens ...... as I notice relaxing further with each breath ...... and I begin to imagine ...... standing in a field ...... as I look around the field ...... seeing the soft green grass ...... and feeling the breeze on my face ...... I glance over and standing there in the middle of a field is a hot air balloon ...... and as I imagine walking over to the hot air balloon ...... I imagine the feel of the ground underfoot ...... and as I get nearer I notice the sound of the flames ...... see them soaring high above the basket ...... it's quite a magnificent sight ...... the basket ...... resting on the ground ...... so strong and stable ...... as I notice the smell of the wicker as I walk up and touch the sturdy basket ...... knowing that I can climb inside and go on an exciting journey ...... as I climb inside ...... and inside the basket it is comfortable ...... with seats and cushions ...... and I can just create a comfortable space for myself ...... and imagine the hot air from the flames above rising up into the balloon ...... and as the balloon begins to gently and slowly rise ...... I can see the balloon high above ...... full of warm air ...... just gently gliding upwards ...... away from the normal hustle and bustle of the world ...... into the quiet, space in the sky ...... and as I notice my breathing ...... breathing quite naturally ...... and as I breathe in and out ...... with every breathe I imagine that the hot air balloon is rising ...... gently ascending higher and higher. And as the balloon rising higher and higher ...... I notice that I feel lighter and lighter ...... as if my whole body is floating ...... and I can just let the balloon glide as high as it chooses to go ...... high up into the sky ...... above the trees ...... above the houses so I can look down and see the houses and streets, fields and rivers below me ...... so small and insignificant ...... and with each and every breath, as I drift higher and higher ...... feeling lighter and lighter ...... as my imagination takes me on a journey as I just enjoy this wonderful feeling of lightness, of freedom ...... and I can go wherever I choose ...... to my special place ......

...... and as I enjoy feeling so light and free from the usual constraints and can see things from a different perspective ...... I am just going to allow myself to re-examine a negative thought I have been believing in the past ...... and in this receptive state I can re-evaluate whether it is actually true ...... I can experience how I feel when I do believe the negative thought to be true ...... and I can experience how I feel if I believe it is not true ...... as I just allow my mind to become aware of the negative thought I am ready and willing to re-evaluate ...... and I wonder ...... is it true? ...... and I wonder ...... can I be 100 per cent sure it's true? ...... and I wonder ...... how do I feel when I believe this to be true? ...... and I wonder ...... how do I feel when I believe it not to be true? ...... as I ask my unconscious mind to help me reassess the validity of this thought ...... is it helpful to me? ...... as I realize I do not need to hold onto this belief ...... and it may not even be true ...... and so I will allow my unconscious mind to make positive changes to allow me to just let it go ...... as I realize I no longer need to focus on it ...... and I realize how good it feels to see it in its true perspective ...... and I will notice how much easier it is for me to challenge thoughts ...... and see a different point of view ...... as my thinking naturally expands ...... and positive thoughts become my natural pattern ...... because I realize they are so much more useful to me ......

...... and I am now so deeply relaxed ...... and comfortable ...... and just enjoying a time when there is nothing of any importance for me to do ...... I can just be ...... and my mind is so receptive to my inner communications that everything I communicate now ...... in this deeply relaxed state ...... will help me in a positive way in my everyday life ...... and as a result of my inner rest and rejuvenation I will feel healthy and full of vitality ...... I will feel confident and optimistic ...... looking forward to things in life ...... but also enjoying the here and now ...... and these good feelings will grow and develop as my levels of confidence increase and I feel really good about myself ...... really enjoying being me ...... when I do resume my normal everyday waking state I will notice that I feel good and have all the energy I need to do all the things I have to do but also all the energy I need to do all the things I want to do ...... as I notice more positive things in life ...... and I will feel confident and optimistic ...... relaxed and calm ......

Only as soon as I am ready ...... and my unconscious mind has finished any processing ...... I will naturally return to a normal alert level of consciousness ...... I will become aware of my physical body ...... as I notice becoming aware of the sounds around me ...... aware of every part of me being awake ...... I am once again becoming aware of where I am ...... and the things around me ...... just as soon as I am ready my eyes will gently open and *every part of me is back here in the present* ...... I am aware of the outside world around me ...... I am aware of feeling great ...... refreshed ...... rejuvenated ......

and so I will just allow my eyes to open as soon as I am ready ...... to just allow my eyes to open ...... gently in my own time ...... feeling refreshed ...... rejuvenated ...... relaxed and calm ...... looking forward ...... feeling positive and full of energy ......

MAIN POINTS

▶ Once you have achieved an altered state of hypnosis focus on a negative thought or belief that you are ready to challenge.
▶ Ask your unconscious mind to consider if it is true, whether you can be 100% sure it is true, how you feel when you believe it to be true, how you feel when you believe it not to be true.
▶ Communicate positive suggestions.
▶ Return to a normal alert state.

THINGS TO REMEMBER

▶ Scientific research indicates that optimism is a positive psychological trait that can lead to increased happiness and well-being. Optimism can be learned. The best way to become more optimistic is to challenge negative thoughts, which may have become habitual. Reassessing negative thinking patterns in self-hypnosis allows you effectively to develop a more positive style of thinking that can have profound beneficial effects on your everyday levels of happiness and well-being.

19

Enhancing creativity

In this chapter you will learn:
* *techniques to increase your creativity.*

Self-hypnosis is a beautiful way of exploring your creativity, whether this is for personal reasons or as a way of expanding your mind to assist with creative tasks, such as writing, art, dance or music.

Research has shown the more positive a person's mood, the higher their creativity. Although creative people come from all walks of life, they all seem to have one thing in common; they love what they are doing. Positive mood and creativity are synonymous; they both lead to each other. Positive mood has been shown to be an antecedent to creativity and occur as a direct consequence of creativity. Indeed, Albert Einstein called his 1907 general theory of relativity 'the happiest thought of my life'.

Increasing the amount of positive thoughts and emotions you experience can benefit you in many ways. Positive thoughts have been shown to produce more flexible and broader thinking patterns, resulting in more creativity.

Insight
Writers' block, which is experienced not just by writers but can affect anyone, refers to the feeling that inspiration is lacking – you can't feel it. In fact it can affect you in many lines of work or in pleasure activities, including relationships or decision making. Feeling blocked is often because the process has become too conscious.

Because consciousness – the ability to verbalize thought and high level thinking – is one aspect that differentiates humans from animals, it is put on a pedestal and considered superior. However, unconscious processing is much more creative and in some ways more valuable. Creativity often stems from the unconscious mind and is then interpreted with the conscious part of your brain and the two work together to create the art, whether it be music, poetry, dance or photography, kicking a football, solving a problem at work, or deciding on a major decision in life. All these things involve creative thinking. The feeling when you have created something special or have made the right decision is an unconscious knowing, which is experienced in a similar way to intuition and is created by similar parts of the brain. You often experience this as a sense, a sort of physical sense, because the unconscious mind communicates in a different way. The unconscious mind is non-verbal. Instead of limiting its use this expands it. The creative part of your mind can be accessed through self-hypnosis.

Predictability diminishes creativity. The conscious mind prefers order and patterns and develops global thinking patterns that are rigid and inflexible. This is useful because it allows us to cope with the vast amount of information coming into our senses at any one time. However, in the state of self-hypnosis you are no longer bound by the constraints of rigid, inflexible thinking. When in self-hypnosis you can allow your mind to drift. In this state it is common to experience original thought. Your unconscious mind contains a vast amount of material and resources that remain untapped in the normal alert state.

Insight

A mathematician once described his own mathematical thinking as largely wordless, often accompanied by mental images that represent the entire solution to a problem. Many mathematicians and physicists agree. The end-product of creativity may be verbal and conscious but the process is often unconscious and non-verbal.

Feelings are so important. I am not talking about emotions but feelings. You can feel you know something – it is on the tip of your tongue. This is such an interesting phenomenon because you have a sense of knowing that you know it but you cannot recall it at that precise moment. This feeling of knowing is the aspect that is interesting – it is the unconscious mind communicating. Developing your recognition of this feeling within self-hypnosis will allow you to recognize experiencing it more in your everyday life. This can lead to the kind of eureka moment we all have when something just occurs to us. Sudden spontaneity is a facet of creativity.

Creativity can be explained by five stages of processing:

1 preparation – consciously thinking about an issue
2 incubation – unconscious processing
3 intimation – a feeling emerges that a solution is on its way
4 insight – the creative idea comes into conscious awareness
5 verification – the idea is consciously thought about, elaborated, and then applied.

Stages 2 and 3 are unconscious processes and self-hypnosis allows you to create a brain state conducive to creativity.

Creativity stems from the very basic parts of the brain, the cerebellum, which modulates activity in the whole brain. Self-hypnosis may also encourage creativity through the right hemisphere of the brain being more dominant. This is an oversimplification of hemisphere differences, but encouraging right brain visual and emotional thinking over left brain logical and analytical thought occurs in hypnosis and is conducive to creativity.

Although, simply spending time in the altered state of consciousness experienced in hypnosis encourages creativity in itself, you can also use self-hypnosis specifically to produce creativity, if you so wish. I have paired this technique with the lift technique. This is excellent for creating a deep state of self-hypnosis in which you can access the unconscious part of your mind and you can control the depth of altered state.

Script for increasing creativity

As I close my eyes ...... and allow myself to consider how pleasant it is ...... just to rest my eyes ...... and allow myself to experience a time of quiet ...... a quiet time just for me ...... and I can allow my imagination to take me on a journey ...... I see a door in front of me ...... the door to a lift ...... and I press the button to call the lift ...... I imagine where the lift could take me ...... on a journey deep inside my mind ...... into my unconscious mind ...... to a place where I feel totally calm and relaxed ...... to a place where I feel safe and secure ...... and as the lift arrives and I hear the sound of the doors opening I look inside the lift ...... as the doors gently open ...... and I notice how warm and comfortable it looks inside ...... and I walk into the

lift and look around ...... I notice a dial with numbers lit up from 10
to 0 ...... I press the button indicating 0 and as the doors close gently
in front of me ...... I enjoy the feeling of shutting out the external
world ...... enjoying this special journey down into my special world
...... feeling comfortable and safe ...... and as the lift begins to move
down ...... as the numbers descend ...... as each floor passes I
am aware of drifting deeper and deeper ...... feeling more and more
comfortable ...... as the numbers descend ...... 10 ...... 9 ...... 8 ......
7 ...... with each floor passing allowing me to relax even further ......
6 ...... 5 ...... 4 ...... as the lift moves smoothly down ...... 3 ......
2 ...... 1 ...... all the way down past 1 to floor 0 ...... and as the lift
gently rests at floor 0 ...... and the door slowly opens I step out into
a corridor ...... with doors on either side ...... and I can just rest here
a moment while I consider ...... and enjoy this unique state of feeling
both so relaxed and yet still awake ...... I recognize that in some ways
this resembles those moments in life where thoughts can just pop
into my mind ...... I don't need to think about them ...... they just
appear ...... because I allow them to appear ...... and so I can choose
to let my unconscious mind work on an issue ...... as I allow myself
to become aware ...... just for a moment ...... of a concept I wish to
develop ...... or a problem I am working on ...... and once I have
considered this for only a moment I can just put it to one side ...... in
fact I can imagine a box ...... a safe place ...... to put that conscious
thought in ...... it can just stay there because it is not required for
my mind to work at a deeper more creative level ...... and I can just
drift deeper into my inner self ...... into my inner unconscious mind
...... the part of me that does not need words ...... or rules ...... it
is flexible and open ...... and so I can go on an exploration of my
creative mind ...... as I imagine walking down the corridor with
doors on each side ...... and I wonder what is behind those doors
...... I wonder what exciting and interesting things lie beyond sight
...... and I can open any door I choose and walk through the door
...... and allow myself to experience whatever is behind that door
...... and I may be surprised ...... I may find a pleasant memory from
the past ...... or an exciting opportunity for the future ...... I can
just allow my imagination to take me wherever it chooses ...... to
explore ...... and I can just learn to recognize my feelings ...... I do
not have to think ...... just to feel ...... and I may feel one door offers
a solution ...... a feeling of knowing ...... and this feeling of knowing
feels pleasant ...... and I notice I feel a buzz of energy ...... joy ......

happiness ...... accompanying this feeling of knowing I know ......
it doesn't matter what it is I know ...... but I can feel this sense of
knowing ...... and I can just let my intuition guide me ...... and I may
notice I suddenly have insight ...... my conscious mind recognizes a
new way of thinking ...... a new idea ...... and this may come now or
may come later ...... when I am in my normal waking state ...... as
my unconscious mind works away all the time ...... even when I busy
doing other things ......

I now feel so deeply relaxed ...... so deeply comfortable ...... that
my mind ...... is so receptive to what I say ...... and I am so deeply
relaxed and comfortable that everything I say to myself can help
me in positive ways in my life ...... as all these thoughts will sink
into my unconscious mind ...... the part of me that knows ...... and
understands ...... and I will notice positive changes in my life ......
because I am ready for them to happen ...... as each day goes by ......
I will feel physically stronger ...... and fitter in every way ...... I will
notice feeling more alert ...... I will feel enthusiastic ...... I will feel
motivated to do all the things I have to do ...... I will feel motivated
to do all the things I want to do ...... I will focus easily ...... as I feel
more optimistic ...... more energetic ...... than I have felt in a long,
long while ...... feeling really good about myself ...... feeling really
good about the possibilities ...... enjoying being me ......

And I wonder what new things I will choose to do ...... as I feel I
have all the energy to do all the things I have to do ...... and I have all
the energy I need to do all the things I want to do ...... as I realize I
have time ...... that I can feel calm and relaxed ...... and I will notice
that my relationships with other people are easy and pleasurable ......
as I am cheerful and content ...... enjoying and looking forward to
the opportunities ahead ...... feeling calm ...... feeling strong ......
as I wake up refreshed and alert each morning ...... after a deep
refreshed sleep ...... feeling optimistic and cheerful ......

And these feelings of calm will allow me to be creative in my thinking
...... as new possibilities emerge ...... and naturally I will expand my
world ...... and develop much more belief in myself ...... and I am
now so deeply relaxed ...... and comfortable ...... and just enjoying a
time when there is nothing of any importance for me to do ...... I can
just be ...... and my mind is so receptive to my inner communications
that everything I communicate now ...... in this deeply relaxed state

...... will help me in a positive way in my everyday life ...... and as a result of my inner rest and rejuvenation I will feel healthy and full of vitality ...... I will feel confident and optimistic ...... looking forward to things in life ...... but also enjoying the here and now ...... and these good feelings will grow and develop as my levels of confidence increase and I feel really good about myself ...... really enjoying being me ...... when I do resume my normal everyday waking state I will notice that I feel good and have all the energy I need to do all the things I have to do but also all the energy I need to do all the things I want to do ...... as I notice more positive things in life ...... and I will feel confident and optimistic ...... relaxed and calm ......

When I am ready ...... and only then ...... and when my unconscious mind has finished any processing ...... I will naturally return to a normal alert level of consciousness ...... I will become aware of my physical body ...... as I notice becoming aware of the sounds around me ...... aware of every part of me being awake ...... and aware of the things around me ...... just as soon as I am ready my eyes will gently open and I will be aware that *every part of me is back here in the present* ...... I am once again becoming aware of where I am ...... I am aware of the outside world around me ...... I am aware of feeling great ...... refreshed ...... rejuvenated ...... and so I will just allow my eyes to open as soon as I am ready ...... just allow my eyes to open ...... gently in my own time ...... feeling refreshed ...... rejuvenated ...... relaxed and calm ...... looking forward ...... feeling positive and full of energy ......

THINGS TO REMEMBER

▶ Creativity stems from and induces positive feelings of well-being.

▶ Creativity comes from unconscious processing and self-hypnosis allows you to enter an altered state of consciousness in which you can function at this creative level.

20

Self-acceptance

In this chapter you will learn:
- *techniques for accepting oneself*
- *techniques for feeling free.*

Wisdom from all cultures and research from Positive Psychology shows us that to be happy you have to happy with yourself. It is not important to 'be' anything specific but to be authentic. Self-acceptance is an important facet to positive psychological well-being. Self-acceptance is about accepting all aspects of yourself; the positive as well as the perceived negative. In fact full self-acceptance is about not judging yourself as positive or negative but just accepting yourself fully. However, during the process of self-acceptance you may find it useful to explore the positive parts of you. Acknowledging positive parts of yourself may be harder than admitting seemingly negative aspects. Often people are naturally harsh on themselves. In a state of self-hypnosis you will find it easier to allow yourself to feel positive about yourself as the critical part of your thinking is reduced.

Accepting oneself technique

When in a relaxed state of self-hypnosis and prior to returning to a normal waking state allow your mind to focus on your pleasant place. Create your own special place where you feel safe and secure. Think of something you really love. It may be a person or an experience; anything that you feel a great sense of love for. It could be a child, a partner, a sibling, or maybe a piece of music, an activity or hobby. Allow yourself to experience the positive feelings you have; feelings of warmth, tenderness, joy, acceptance, excitement, understanding, unconditional love. Examine the things you love about this thing or person. Then allow yourself to realize that they are not perfect, as nothing is perfect. Acknowledge that these apparent imperfections do not detract from the love you feel. They may even add to it. As you fully accept and appreciate the person or thing and love it fully. Become aware of the positive feelings generated in your physical body, perhaps a warm feeling in your stomach or chest. Allow these good feelings to develop, visualize them pulsating through your body, send positive messages all through your body. You may visualize colours, make these as vibrant as possible, you may even hear sound. Using these powerful feelings of unconditional love and joy focus on yourself, as a person, and direct these good feelings toward yourself. Accept yourself in the same way that you accept other people and experiences you love. Experience this deep and unconditional love towards yourself. When in self-hypnosis positive thoughts are much more plentiful because there are fewer stress hormones circulating round the body and brain. This makes feeling positively towards yourself much easier as the critical part of your brain is subdued in this state. Research shows that experiencing these positive emotions during a state of self-hypnosis makes them more likely to occur in your everyday life. I have paired this technique with a count down technique as this allows you to drift as deeply as you choose within self-hypnosis which facilitates the self-acceptance technique.

Script for self-acceptance

As I focus on my breathing …… in and out …… just slowing down with each breath …… and I can just lie (or sit) here …… enjoying a bit of time for me …… some space for me …… just to relax …… and I can allow my imagination to drift …… as I imagine I am standing at the top of a beautiful staircase …… and I can imagine the stairs in front of me …… stretching down …… I can feel the banister as my hand rests upon it …… and I feel safe and secure …… standing at the top of this staircase …… and my mind imagines where the staircase is taking me to …… to a place where I feel safe and comfortable …… relaxed …… into my own inner world …… where I feel completely comfortable …… and in a moment I am going to walk down the stairs, one step at a time …… and with each step down the stairs …… I will notice that

I feel more and more relaxed …… allowing myself to go deeper and deeper into a beautiful state of deep relaxation and hypnosis …… I will begin to count down from 10 to 1 and with each descending number I will take one step down the stairs …… with each descending number I will find myself becoming one tenth or ten per cent even more absorbed …… with each descending number and each step down the stairs I will feel more and more deeply relaxed …… (*begin counting down slowly and silently from 10 to 1 and imagine yourself walking down the stairs, one step at a time*) 10 …… 9 …… and with each step down I allow myself to drift deeper …… 8 …… deeper and deeper …… 7 …… as very pleasant sensations of safety and comfort spread down through my body …… 6 …… with every breath just letting go …… 5 …… deeper and deeper still …… 4 …… I notice as I go down the stairs how distant I feel …… entering into my own world …… 3 …… 2 …… all the way down into my special place …… a place just for me …… where I feel safe and secure …… happy and relaxed …… all the way down …… deeper and deeper …… 1 …… and as I reach the bottom step …… and step off I can continue to allow myself to drift even deeper …… as deep as I choose to go …… all the way …… as deep as I choose …… and I can just allow myself to drift just as deep as I wish …… imagining what it would be like to go down past 1 …… down to 0 …… and even down into minus numbers …… all the way …… down to minus 1 …… minus 5 …… minus 10 …… even down to minus 50 …… minus 100 …… as my mind can take me on a special journey wherever it wants me to go …… to a pleasant place …… all the way …… deeper and deeper ……

And I just allow myself to consider something or someone that I love …… and I examine these feelings of love …… and allow myself to experience them …… and I wonder what it is that makes me love so deeply …… and as I think of something or someone I love I notice feelings of warmth develop …… tenderness …… joy …… and the love feels so tangible as if I could grasp hold of it …… so real …… as the joy sweep through me …… and as I consider that this is completely unconditional …… it just is …… whatever …… whenever …… forever …… and it feels so good to rest for a moment and appreciate that love that I feel …… and the warm feelings that accompany it …… and as I allow myself to experience this feeling of love …… and ponder on …… how I feel this love …… what colour it is …… how it feels to me …… what images come to mind ……

maybe even symbolic images …… that just appear …… representing the enormity of unconditional love …… and as I feel the sensation of love and joy cascading through my body …… and I can even visualize that love …… see the colours and shapes develop …… and I realize that it is easy to direct all these good feelings toward myself …… and a sense of unconditional love develops …… as I realize I can accept myself totally and love myself unconditionally …… as I am gentle with myself as I am others …… and I can just rest and enjoy these good feelings …… as I feel so calm and relaxed …… and full of love …… unconditional love …… and I realize that there are positive things I like about myself …… and I can just be me …… I don't have to be anything …… I can just be me …… and that's fine …… and I can love me …… for exactly who I am …… and it feels so liberating to just accept myself …… so easy to love myself …… totally …… and just be …… as I feel those vibrant colours and warmth cascading through me …… into every part of me ……

…… and I am now so deeply relaxed …… and comfortable …… and just enjoying a time when there is nothing of any importance for me to do …… I can just be …… and my mind is so receptive to my inner communications that everything I communicate now …… in this deeply relaxed state …… will help me in a positive way in my everyday life …… and as a result of my inner rest and rejuvenation I will feel healthy and full of vitality …… I will feel confident and optimistic …… looking forward to things in life …… but also enjoying the here and now …… and these good feelings will grow and develop as my levels of confidence increase and I feel really good about myself …… really enjoying being me …… when I do resume my normal everyday waking state I will notice that I feel good and have all the energy I need to do all the things I have to do but also all the energy I need to do all the things I want to do …… as I notice more positive things in life …… and I will feel confident and optimistic …… relaxed and calm ……

Only as soon as I am ready …… and my unconscious mind has finished any processing …… I will naturally return to a normal alert level of consciousness …… I will become aware of my physical body …… as I notice becoming aware of the sounds around me …… aware of every part of me being awake …… I am once again becoming aware of where I am …… and the things around me …… just as soon as I am ready my eyes will gently open and *every part of me is back here in the present*

...... I am aware of the outside world around me ...... I am aware of feeling great ...... refreshed ...... rejuvenated ...... and so I will just allow my eyes to open as soon as I am ready ...... to just allow my eyes to open ...... gently in my own time ...... feeling refreshed ...... rejuvenated ...... relaxed and calm ...... looking forward ...... feeling positive and full of energy ......

MAIN POINTS

▶ Once you have achieved an altered state of hypnosis focus on something or someone you really love.
▶ Allow yourself to experience the positive feelings you have; feelings of warmth, tenderness, joy, acceptance, excitement, understanding, unconditional love.
▶ Become aware of the positive feelings generated in your physical body.
▶ Focus these powerful feelings of unconditional love and joy towards yourself.
▶ Communicate positive suggestions.
▶ Return to a normal alert state.

Experiencing freedom technique

A further way to develop self-acceptance is to let go of old, redundant feelings towards yourself and emerge afresh. This is a beautiful technique that uses the analogy of emerging out of a cocoon like a butterfly. Often in hypnosis analogies are used because the unconscious mind excels at processing non-verbal information. Visualizing yourself breaking out of a cocoon and emerging as a beautiful butterfly can be used to help you develop a sense of possibility, of positive change. Accepting oneself does not mean remaining the same. Change and development are always possible and having a psychological fresh start, a clean slate, can allow you to feel differently towards yourself in your everyday life.

Script for freedom technique

As I allow myself to consider the possibility of just being ...... not having to do anything ...... I can just be ...... and as I consider this possibility I can just allow my eyes to close ...... and I can imagine there ...... in front of me ...... a beautiful pool with crystal clear water ...... as I notice the colours and shapes rippling gently across the surface of the pool ...... it looks so inviting ...... and as I imagine just dipping my toe into the water ...... and I feel the water against my skin ...... I realize it is beautifully warm ...... soft against my skin ...... as I step into the pool and feel the warm water caressing my ankles ...... and as the warm water rises up ...... as I step deeper into the pool I notice that my body is beginning to feel so relaxed ...... as the warm water covers my lower legs ...... my legs feel so pleasantly relaxed ...... and these feelings of relaxation in my legs ...... continue to travel up my body as the warm water envelops my lower body ...... over my knees ...... up to my thighs ...... and my legs feel warm ...... and so deeply relaxed ...... as all the unnecessary tension just drifts out of my body ...... as my muscles let go of any tension ...... as it just melts away ...... and as I glide even deeper into the warm water and the water drifts up to my waist ...... and then I sink even deeper in the water up to my chest and back ...... and as I submerge my hands in the water and then my arms ...... and I can just allow myself to lie back in the warm water ...... floating quite naturally ...... and I am surprised at how easy it is just to let go and let my body float effortlessly in the water ...... so deeply relaxed all through my body ...... and with every in-breath I breathe in feelings of calmness ...... and serenity ...... and with every out-breath ...... as I allow myself to float ...... feeling so deeply relaxed and comfortable ...... and I let my mind drift to a special place ......

...... as these feeling of deep relaxation continue ...... and I can become as deeply relaxed as I choose to be ...... as I feel safe and comfortable in my special place ...... and as my body feels so relaxed and warm I can just imagine a cocoon forming around my physical body ...... allowing me to relax even more deeply ......

...... I am aware that life is full of possibilities ...... of new things ...... which I may not even have thought of yet ...... and so as I relax even further and allow my mind and body just to drift ...... and I consider the idea that in some ways I have been constrained by some feelings towards myself in the past ...... and yet I no longer need to be ...... I can break free from old thinking habits of the past that are no longer useful to me and I can think about myself in positive ways ...... and as I imagine further the cocoon forming around me ...... wrapping itself round me ...... layers and layers ...... allowing me to enter into an even deeper state of relaxation ...... as I feel the folds of the cocoon enveloping my whole body ...... and I feel so safe and warm ...... within my cocoon ...... and I can just allow the inner me to rest for a moment and consider for a moment the possibility of starting afresh ...... as I know that life is full of change ...... and although change can sometimes be a challenge it is also an opportunity ...... an opportunity to feel differently ...... to think differently ...... to act differently ...... as I consider who I would like to be ...... how I would like to feel about myself ...... as I accept that I grow and develop and change ...... and that some old patterns of thinking may no longer be useful to me ...... but that I do not have to be constrained by old habits ...... I can be free to be ...... and so within the safety and comfort of my cocoon I can realize that I am just me ...... and I can be me ...... and I will rest here a moment and just be ......

...... and ask my unconscious mind to consider any aspects of my thoughts that are no longer useful to me ...... and which I can break free of here and now ...... today ...... and how good I will feel knowing that I can be free from any of these old, redundant thinking patterns of the past ...... I will allow all these pleasant positive feelings develop ...... as I look forward to the future ...... look forward to all the possibilities ...... and when I am ready I can just allow the cocoon to start to break open ...... and unfurl ...... slowly opening up ...... as I know I am now ready to emerge ...... to break free ...... ready to emerge with all those positive feelings ...... feeling really good about myself ......

...... really enjoying being me ...... and as I become aware of the cocoon breaking away ...... and I feel myself emerging ...... just a bit at a time ...... slowly emerging ...... rejuvenated ...... revitalized ...... refreshed ...... like a beautiful butterfly ...... I can spread my wings ...... and fly away ...... soaring up into the sky ...... rising higher and higher ...... with a sense of freedom ...... soaring high and free ...... seeing things from a new perspective ...... new possibilities ...... and I wonder what the first new thing I will do will be ...... how I feel so good about myself ...... feel so good about all the positive possibilities ...... as I just allow my mind to drift away and I imagine rising higher and higher ...... spreading my wings even further ...... as I soar higher and higher.

...... and I am now so deeply relaxed ...... and comfortable ...... and just enjoying a time when there is nothing of any importance for me to do …… I can just be …… and my mind is so receptive to my inner communications that everything I communicate now …… in this deeply relaxed state …… will help me in a positive way in my everyday life …… and as a result of my inner rest and rejuvenation I will feel healthy and full of vitality …… I will feel confident and optimistic …… looking forward to things in life …… but also enjoying the here and now …… and these good feelings will grow and develop as my levels of confidence increase and I feel really good about myself …… really enjoying being me …… when I do resume my normal everyday waking state I will notice that I feel good and have all the energy I need to do all the things I have to do but also all the energy I need to do all the things I want to do …… as I notice more positive things in life …… and I will feel confident and optimistic …… relaxed and calm ……

…… Only as soon as I am ready …… and my unconscious mind has finished any processing …… I will naturally return to a normal alert level of consciousness …… I will become aware of my physical body …… as I notice becoming aware of the sounds around me …… aware of every part of me being awake …… I am once again becoming aware of where I am …… and the things around me …… just as soon as I am ready my eyes will gently open and *every part of me is back here in the present* …… I am aware of the outside world around me …… I am aware of feeling great …… refreshed …… rejuvenated …… and so I will just allow my eyes to open as soon as I am ready …… to just allow my eyes to open …… gently in my own time …… feeling refreshed …… rejuvenated …… relaxed and calm …… looking forward …… feeling positive and full of energy ……

MAIN POINTS

▶ Once you have achieved an altered state of hypnosis form a cocoon around yourself.
▶ Consider the possibility of starting afresh.
▶ Break out of the cocoon and experience emerging like a beautiful butterfly.
▶ Become aware of the positive feelings of freedom generated in your physical body.
▶ Communicate positive suggestions.
▶ Return to a normal alert state.

THINGS TO REMEMBER

▶ Self-acceptance is an important facet of positive psychological well-being. Specific techniques can be used within self-hypnosis to encourage a positive self-acceptance which can lead to increased self-esteem and psychological well-being in your everyday life.

Part 5
Self-hypnosis for better life-physical well-being

21

Psychological well-being
and health

In this chapter you will learn:
* *how the mind and the body are interlinked*
* *how hypnotherapy can contribute to physical health.*

A wealth of evidence shows us that psychological well-being plays
a vital role in physical health and well-being. The previous chapters
focused on improving and maintaining a sense of positive well-being
through increasing positive states of mind. Positive psychological
well-being has been shown to be associated with many health
benefits. Positive emotions (such as emotional well-being, positive
mood, joy and happiness) and positive traits (such as life satisfaction,
hopefulness, motivation and optimism) are associated with increased
physical well-being.

Hypnotherapy is a psychological therapy with a biological basis.
In other words the mind affects the body and in turn the body
affects the mind. Hypnotherapy is therefore beneficial in many
areas of emotional and physical health. It is a scientifically based
mind–body therapy. One of the most amazing discoveries of modern
psychobiology is the new system of molecular communication
between brain and body at the cellular level. We now know
that messages from the brain travel to receiving stations on the
surface of every cell of the body. This is the essence of mind–body
communication.

One of the ways self-hypnosis can help physical health is through the reduction of stress and the symptoms associated with stress. Stress has negative effects on the body and can lead to or exacerbate ill health. Stress can lead to a weakened immune system and other health risks such as high blood pressure. Self-hypnosis is therefore useful in maintaining good health and in protecting the body from stress-related disorders.

Self-hypnosis can also be beneficial in other physical matters, particularly those of sleep and weight. Being of a healthy weight, sleeping well and coping with stress are all beneficial to your overall health and well-being. These represent interactions between the mind and body and you can use self-hypnosis to help to lose weight and sleep better, and to feel less stressed. Self-hypnosis can also help you maintain a healthy immune system through mind–body interactions.

The psychology of health and disease

Health is about balance and equilibrium of the mind and body. The psychology and physiology of an individual are interdependent and the mind affects the body continuously and therefore has a role to play in all areas of health and well-being. Self-hypnosis can enhance your physical well-being and help you maintain a good state of physical health.

Although research shows it can be of benefit in many physical conditions, self-hypnosis is not an appropriate cure for illness. This is within the practice of professional clinical hypnotherapy, not self-hypnosis. You should always consult your doctor if you have any signs or symptoms you are concerned about. Never use self-hypnosisfor a medical condition.

How the mind contributes to physical symptoms

The mind and body are intrinsically linked through chemical messages which are produced in the brain and body in response to emotions, feelings, thoughts and beliefs. Thoughts can create physical changes.

Insight
Thoughts that are most prevalent become reality.

The interaction between the mind and body is demonstrated in the placebo effect. This is where an inert substance causes an effect. The reaction occurs because the person *thinks* the substance contains an active ingredient. Their thoughts and beliefs cause the body to react as it would if the substance were real. For example, a group of participants were told they were testing two new drugs, a tranquilizer and a stimulant. They were given either two red or two blue tablets. Participants consistently reported that the red tablets had stimulating effects and blue tablets made them feel relaxed. Both were placebo – they were sugar pills with no active ingredients. Thinking they had taken a tablet that was going to have a certain effect caused the effect to happen. The colour of the tablets added to this effect because of the associations we have with those colours.

In another experiment volunteers were given harmless but painful electric shocks. Half the subjects were told that an anti-pain cream had been applied. These subjects reported less pain. In fact the cream applied contained no active ingredients and therefore should have had no effect. They thought they would feel less pain and therefore they did feel less pain.

Thoughts can alleviate symptoms and produce symptoms. This has been shown in a study in which a large group of subjects vomited when they believed they had been given a substance that caused vomiting. In fact the substance was water. Vomiting was caused by the subjects *thinking* they would vomit. This belief had a physical effect on the body.

But how does this happen? Thoughts originate from chemical signals in the brain. Thoughts also cause chemicals to be produced in the brain. These chemicals send messages to the body. The belief that this group of people had that they were going to vomit made their brains send messages to their bodies to induce vomiting.

Phantom pregnancy (pseudocyesis) is another good example of the power of the mind. In this condition a woman believes she is pregnant and displays symptoms of pregnancy, for example breast tenderness, bloating of the abdomen and even morning sickness. These seemingly physical symptoms reinforce her belief and the symptoms are maintained. The physical body is responding to thoughts.

How hypnotherapy can be beneficial in physical well-being

Hypnotherapy is particularly effective in maintaining good physical health as it is based on the interaction between the mind and body. Self-hypnosis allows you to have more control over your thoughts and beliefs which can then have positive effects on your health and physical well-being. Self-hypnosis has also been shown to reduce stress and the corresponding negative effects of stress on the body and immune system functioning.

The role of the mind in disease

The role of the mind is particularly relevant in chronic conditions. The brain gets used to sending messages to the body which cause symptoms and it becomes habitual. Irritable bowel syndrome (IBS) is a good example of this. Often a person experiences pain, bloating and irregular bowel movements during a period of illness or stress and the brain continues to send these signals long after the original organic illness dissipates. The individual can become anxious that the symptoms will continue and this anxiety prolongs the symptoms. The symptoms can be the result of habitual thoughts which cause the body to react as if there were a physical cause. This explains why physical treatment is not effective. For the symptoms to be resolved it is the thought patterns and beliefs that need to be addressed. In the normal conscious state it is difficult to retrain the brain not to believe these symptoms are real. However, hypnosis allows new ways of learning and more appropriate thoughts to be created much more easily. In hypnosis the belief system surrounding symptoms can be effectively challenged and new beliefs can be reinforced. This can then break the cycle of thought patterns which previously have served to reinforce the experience of physical symptoms. Clinical hypnosis is recognized as one of the most effective treatments for IBS. However, IBS is not suitable for treatment with self-hypnosis and it is important that you consult a professional clinical hypnotherapist for treatment regarding IBS.

Insight

For any physical health issue it is important to consult with your doctor who will be able to advise you on seeking help from a professional clinical hypnotherapist.

THINGS TO REMEMBER

▶ Psychoneuroimmunology, the scientific study of how the mind and body interact in relation to health and the immune system, provides a wealth of evidence that thoughts and beliefs affect the physical body. Placebo research provided additional evidence showing how powerful thoughts can be in relation to physical symptoms. Stress can have negative effects on the immune system. Self-hypnosis can be beneficial in reducing the negative impact of stress and producing positive thoughts and beliefs that have beneficial effects on health and well-being. It can be used to help you develop a healthy pattern of behaviour in relation to eating and sleep, two basic fundamentals of health and can also help you create an optimum state of physical health through enhancing immune functioning.

22

Stress

In this chapter you will learn:
- *about the effects on the body of negative thinking and stress*
- *techniques for assisting you to cope with stress*
- *techniques for assisting the body's immune functioning.*

Negative thoughts and their effect on the body

Negative thinking is accompanied by and contributes to stress. Stress has both psychological and physical consequences. Stress leads to an increase in the production of cortisol, the stress hormone. Chronic stress leads to an overproduction of this hormone which can lead to a suppression of the immune system. Stress is one of the common reasons a person visits their GP with over half of GP appointments being stress related and many physical illnesses are exacerbated by stress.

Negative emotions including stress and anxiety have been shown to increase susceptibility to a range of other health-related conditions including asthma and allergies. Evidence shows that people with diagnosed symptoms of stress are over half more likely to require additional health support than people without these symptoms. This is most likely due to the effect stress has on weakening the immune system.

Insight
Stress has also been linked to obesity and the many health problems connected with putting extra strain on the body from carrying extra weight. People find it much more difficult to lose weight if their system is unbalanced due to stress.

How the brain perceives stress and how people cope affects their physiological response. Therefore controlling stress responses through self-hypnosis can help with the progression of disease and healing of the body. As we cannot easily change the amount of stress someone encounters, we need to reduce the negative effect stress has on the brain and body. This is what self-hypnosis can do. Regular periods of self-hypnosis can lead to a reduction in stress levels sufficient to protect the immune system.

Insight

Stress is the modern bug of society. Many people suffer from feelings of stress and the symptoms associated with being stressed. Sometimes these symptoms can be severe and require professional help.

In cases of severe anxiety or any form of mental health problem it is important that you talk to your doctor. They may recommend seeking professional help from a professional clinical hypnotherapist. Self-hypnosis is not advised in these cases.

Often stress begins as a reaction to an uncontrollable event or series of events in your life. It can be accompanied by a feeling of helplessness – that you cannot change things because they are uncontrollable.

Sometimes it is necessary to make changes in your life, but recognizing this and being able to make the right decision requires a different way of thinking. Conscious thought is often rigid. Unconscious processing is much more flexible. Accessing the unconscious part of your mind while in hypnosis can allow you to find new solutions and new ways of coping with the pressures of everyday life. Often just a small change can make a considerable difference to your life. Being ready to change and having the insight to see the right changes to make is difficult while feeling the effects of stress. Self-hypnosis gives your mind a window of opportunity to be creative in deciding what you could change in your life. It also helps you cope better with aspects of your life that you cannot change. Having the ability to cope with everyday stresses and strains as well as more serious stressors in life, like moving house, changing job or relationships, is essential to maintaining a positive state of well-being. Building inner resources to help you deal with everyday events can be helpful. Self-hypnosis can help you do this.

Purely spending time in self-hypnosis has the benefit of naturally reducing stress levels as the body goes into a relaxed state and the parasympathetic nervous system takes over. The brain sends messages to the body that it can reduce the number of stress chemicals it produces and the body can be in a state of natural equilibrium. Spending regular periods in self-hypnosis has an accumulative effect which can allow you to feel calmer in the normal waking state. The body and mind both benefit from these periods of rest which make the brain and body respond better in times of stress.

The biology of stress

Physically the body is well designed to cope with acute major stressors. The natural ability of the body to instigate the 'fight or flight' response prepares the body to cope with acute stress. However in modern day society the majority of stress is accumulative and chronic. Long-term stress leads to an increase in the production of cortisol which can exacerbate problems and leave you feeling on edge and anxious. The amygdala, the fear centre of the brain, becomes overactive and negative thoughts are more likely to enter your conscious awareness.

The psychology of stress

How the body responds to stress is affected by how the event is interpreted. Thoughts and thinking patterns affect whether the body responds in a positive or negative way. Thought processes become habitual and sometimes a change in thinking is beneficial to influence how the body responds to stress. Remember these thought patterns originate from your unconscious mind and therefore self-hypnosis can help you produce different and more helpful thought patterns in your everyday conscious state.

HOW DOES SELF-HYPNOSIS HELP WITH STRESS IN EVERYDAY LIFE?

▶ Physical reduction of stress hormones.
▶ Opportunity for unconscious mind to process information.
▶ Allows for new thought patterns – thoughts affect the body.

Specific techniques

Although simply spending regular periods of time in self-hypnosis is beneficial in itself it is also possible to use specific techniques within self-hypnosis to enable you to cope better with stress and the feelings associated with stress.

Hypnotherapy is based on the principle that your unconscious mind has the resources it needs to initiate change and solve any issues you have identified within yourself that you wish to change. It is not necessary to understand why problems have started and sometimes even when you know it doesn't seem to help you control them. However, it is useful to remember that the unconscious mind is 'on your side', it's not against you, and it is likely that you created any issues or problems as a coping mechanism. Even something which is now a problem behaviour often started as a way of protecting you in some way. Hypnosis is useful because it allows you to re-set this protective mechanism and make changes when things are no longer useful and no longer appropriate to you in your life. To do this it is not always necessary or even advantageous to work out why they started. Hypnosis gives your unconscious mind an opportunity to find more appropriate ways of dealing with things; a way of making a fresh start.

Reducing stress technique script

As I just settle myself down ...... and allow myself some time ...... some time just for me ...... some time just for me to be ...... and there is nothing of any importance I have to do ...... I can just be ...... and the thought of having some space and time for me ...... for me to concentrate on myself ...... allows me to let go of any thoughts about the outside world ...... as I allow my eyes to close ...... and I consider that although breathing is an unconscious process ...... I can have control over my breathing ...... and having control over my breathing allows me to change the way I feel ...... and I allow myself to consider how I would like to feel ...... relaxed and calm ...... and so I can direct these feelings as I begin to notice and control the way I breathe ...... quite naturally ...... as I don't have to force anything

...... I can just notice breathing in through my nose ...... slowly and smoothly ...... and as I do I hear myself saying the word *calm* ...... as I breathe in calmness ...... and as I do I let my whole chest and abdomen fill up with air ...... so my whole body and mind feel calm ...... and then naturally just allow all the air to leave my body as I exhale through my nose ...... slowly and smoothly ...... and as I do I hear myself saying the word *relaxed* ...... as I can just let go ...... and let my body and mind relax all the way through ...... as I expel all the air out of my body ...... and I can just pause until my body indicates to me to breathe in ...... and as I do so ...... breathing slowly and smoothly in through my nose ...... and hearing silently the word *calm* ...... as I breathe in calmness ...... letting my chest and stomach rise ...... filling my body with calmness ...... and then just let it go ...... exhaling slowly and smoothly ...... hearing silently the word ...... *relaxed* ...... as on each out-breath I feel more and more relaxed ...... just letting go ...... and I can continue to just concentrate on my breathing as I naturally breathe slowly and smoothly ...... breathing in feelings of calm and on every out-breath experiencing relaxation spreading down through my body ...... and as I continue to breathe slowly and smoothly I can just allow my mind to drift to a pleasant place ...... a special place ...... where I can just allow myself to relax and feel calm ......

As I settle down and allow myself to realize that I have sometime in the past felt very stressed ...... I get wound up easily ...... I feel irritable ...... and unable to cope ...... and I can imagine these feelings ...... and I can sense them in my body ...... and its okay to acknowledge them ...... here and now in this deeply relaxed state ...... where I am safe ...... and secure ...... and as I recognize the feeling in my body of stress ...... I can give those feelings colour ...... a colour that represents that feeling to me ...... and I can let it develop so it's clear ...... just in its own time ...... and now I recognize that I don't feel this everywhere in my body ...... just in that place ...... and I can recognize that in another part of my body I feel calm and relaxed ...... happy and tranquil ...... and as I experience these feelings I can just give them a colour ...... and see the colour developing in that part of my body ...... whatever colour seems appropriate to me to represent those pleasant feelings of calm ...... and I can just let that colour develop ...... become vibrant ...... clear in my mind ...... and the accompanying good feelings ...... and

I realize that I can let these good feelings and vibrant colour spread out from that part of my body to the rest of my body ...... through the nerves ...... along the blood vessels ...... through my bones ...... all the pathways of my body ...... spreading out to every cell ...... infiltrating every cell of my body with its vibrant colour and pleasant feeling ......

And when I come across the other colour in my body I can just let the new colour wash over it ...... letting it fade away as it's no longer relevant ...... replaced with the new vibrant colour ...... and so too all those positive feelings ...... sweep through my body ...... as my whole body fills with the vibrant colour and pleasant feelings of deep relaxation and calm ...... as the feeling spreads up into my mind ...... allowing me to sink even deeper into this beautiful state of relaxation which I can experience more and more in my everyday life ......

I now feel so deeply relaxed ...... so deeply comfortable ...... that my mind ...... is so receptive to what I say ...... and as I am so deeply relaxed and comfortable that everything I say to myself can help me in positive ways in my life ...... as all these thoughts will sink into my unconscious mind ...... the part of me that knows ...... and understands ...... and I will notice positive changes in my life ...... because I am ready for them to happen ...... as each day goes by ...... I will feel physically stronger ...... and fitter in every way ...... I will notice feeling more alert ...... I will feel enthusiastic ...... I will feel motivated to do all the things I have to do ...... I will feel motivated to do all the things I want to do ...... I will focus easily ...... as I feel more optimistic ...... more energetic ...... than I have felt in a long, long while ...... feeling really good about myself ...... feeling really good about the possibilities ...... enjoying being me ......

And I wonder what new things I will choose to do? ...... as I feel I have all the energy I need to do all the things I have to do ...... and I have all the energy I need to do all the things I want to do ...... as I realize I have time ...... that I can feel calm and relaxed ...... and I will notice that my relationships with other people are easy and pleasurable ...... as I am cheerful and content ...... enjoying and looking forward to the opportunities ahead ...... feeling calm ...... feeling strong ...... as I wake up refreshed and alert each morning ...... after a deep refreshed sleep ...... feeling optimistic and cheerful ......

And these feelings of calm will allow me to be creative in my thinking ...... as new possibilities emerge ...... and naturally I will expand my world ...... and develop much more belief in myself ...... and I am now so deeply relaxed ...... and comfortable ...... and just enjoying a time when there is nothing of any importance for me to do ...... I can just be ...... and my mind is so receptive to my inner communications that everything I communicate now ...... in this deeply relaxed state ...... will help me in a positive way in my everyday life ...... and as a result of my inner rest and rejuvenation I will feel healthy and full of vitality ...... I will feel confident and optimistic ...... looking forward to things in life ...... but also enjoying the here and now ...... and these good feelings will grow and develop as my levels of confidence increase and I feel really good about myself ...... really enjoying being me ...... when I do resume my normal everyday waking state I will notice that I feel good and have all the energy I need to do all the things I have to do but also all the energy I need to do all the things I want to do ...... as I notice more positive things in life ...... and I will feel confident and optimistic ...... relaxed and calm ......

When I am ready ...... and only then ...... and when my unconscious mind has finished any processing ...... I will naturally return to a normal alert level of consciousness ...... I will become aware of my physical body ...... as I notice becoming aware of the sounds around me ...... aware of every part of me being awake ...... and aware of the things around me ...... just as soon as I am ready my eyes will gently open and I will be aware that *every part of me is back here in the present* ...... I am once again becoming aware of where I am ...... I am aware of the outside world around me ...... I am aware of feeling great ...... refreshed ...... rejuvenated ...... and so I will just allow my eyes to open as soon as I am ready ...... just allow my eyes to open ...... gently in my own time ...... feeling refreshed ...... rejuvenated ...... relaxed and calm ...... looking forward ...... feeling positive and full of energy ......

MAIN POINTS

▶ When in a deeply relaxed state allow yourself to consider your stress.
▶ Locate where you feel it in your body and give it a colour.
▶ Locate a part of your body that feels the exact opposite to this, that feels calm and relaxed.

- ▶ Give this part a colour and let the colour and positive feelings develop.
- ▶ Allow this colour and all the positive feelings to flow through your body.
- ▶ Let them override the old feelings of stress and let the new colour replace the old.
- ▶ Let the pleasant feelings flow through your whole body and up to your mind.
- ▶ Communicate positive suggestions.
- ▶ Return to a normal alert state.

Immune functioning

As well as using self-hypnosis to improve psychological well-being and reduce stress it can also be used specifically to improve immune functioning. The immune system is controlled by the hypothalamus. Chronic stress detrimentally affects the hypothalamus and has resulting negative effects on the immune system. Self-hypnosis can enhance the ability of the hypothalamus to work efficient and effectively in controlling the stress response and immune system of your body.

Boosting the immune system

Chronic stress negatively affects the immune system and can lead to susceptibility to minor infections, like a cold or flu, or a reduction in the healing of injuries. Hypnosis can indirectly help the immune system to work more efficiently through reducing stress and its effects. It can also effect healing and recovery directly by enhancing the ability of the immune system to tackle infection and enhance healing.

In sport, hypnosis is used within rehabilitation psychology to help athletes recover from injury. Rehabilitation psychology is concerned with the use of psychological techniques and therapies to facilitate successful rehabilitation following injury. Techniques are employed both to decrease the negative effects of stress and negative thought patterns and to increase the body's own ability to recover through positive therapy. It has also been shown to be useful in helping people recover more quickly following surgery.

SELF-HYPNOSIS AND IMMUNE STRENGTHENING

During hypnosis it is also possible to use techniques to facilitate balance between the mind and body and positively affect physical and mental well-being. These techniques are based on evidence from psychoneuroimmunology, the scientific study of mind–body medicine.

Insight
This is a general technique useful for supporting a healthy immune system. If you suffer from any serious health issues it is important that you consult your doctor and seek professional help.

When you are comfortable in a state of self-hypnosis use the technique described in this script. You may find that it is useful to read the script through a few times just prior to hypnosis and then centre on the main points when you are in a state of self-hypnosis. This is paired with a technique that encourages awareness of the body.

Immune strengthening script

As I gently close my eyes and focus on my breathing, in …… and out …… and while I continue to focus on my breathing I realize there is nothing of importance for me to do …… just to be …… this is my time …… a time just for me …… a time for me to really concentrate on myself …… I am going to just let myself focus on my favourite place in nature …… and it's a beautiful day …… I notice the sky is a special shade of blue, very clear …… it's a warm day …… a warm summer's day …… there is a dazzling sun in the sky …… and …… it's so bright that I just want to relax and enjoying feeling the warmth of the sun on my body ……

…… and surprisingly I find that I can direct the sun's rays over and around my body, and as I realize this, I begin to direct the light from the sun over my face …… I can see its light as a golden stream of bright yellow and orange …… and I can feel the warmth of the light from the sun on my face, just relaxing those muscles across my forehead ...... drifting down around the eyes and the nose and mouth ...... and as I do this, I find that the facial muscles begin to flatten out as they relax, and I let go ...... all the way ...... as the warmth spreads down into my jaw ...... letting go of any tension ......

And it's a beautiful day ...... I move the light from the sun into the throat area ...... feeling the warmth of the sun over my neck, relaxing all those muscles, letting go. And as the sunlight moves down across my shoulders I feel my shoulders letting go of any tension ...... like a weight has been lifted off them ...... I realize how I relaxed I feel, so comfortable and at peace with the world ...... all of my focused attention on the warm feelings of relaxation spreading down through my body ...... and as I direct the light from the sun down the right arm, seeing, feeling the warmth of the sun ...... the glow from the orange beam of light ...... down from the shoulders to the tips of the fingers, the right arm begins to relax and let go, relax and let go ...... and it's a beautiful feeling to be here right now ...... the warmth of the light from the sun penetrates the nerves and bones and muscles of that right arm all the way through ...... it is such a beautiful day ...... as I move the sun over to the left arm and guide the light from the sun down the left arm, from the top of the shoulders all the way down to the tips of the fingers ...... I can feel the left arm relaxing, becoming heavy, and comfortable and relaxed ...... now the light moves across and into the chest area and the chest and all the muscles there relax ...... my breathing deepens quite naturally ...... slow, deep breathing ...... without effort ...... and the relaxation continues down into the abdomen all the way down to my hips and thighs and over to the right leg ...... the beautiful warm sun sinks all the way down the leg ...... relaxing every muscle ...... down to my toes ...... and now down the left leg from the top of the hips all the way down to the tips of my toes ...... I just let go of any tension ...... and it's a beautiful day ...... I am now only aware of how my body feels ...... totally and completely relaxed ...... from the top of my head to the tips of my toes ...... and as I become less aware of my body ...... I realize that I can just forget my physical body ...... as I notice that I am not fully aware of all of my body ...... as it rests so peacefully ...... and I can just forget about it ......

...... and I can just rest here and as my mind relaxes even further I just notice the sun in the sky going down as the day comes to an end ...... with the sun going down ...... further down in the sky ...... deeper and deeper ...... and the sky is ablaze with an abundance of colours of crimson and bright purple and blue yellow streaks ...... and it's a beautiful evening ...... and the sun goes further and further down, over the horizon, until ...... all that is left ...... is a black ...... velvety sky ...... and twinkling up there in the sky is a single twinkling star ...... and I find myself completely engrossed in that one star ...... nothing else matters except this beautiful single solitary sparkling star in the sky ...... and it's a beautiful night ...... apart from the one star it is very dark, but I feel so safe ...... so comfortable ...... so relaxed, and at peace with the universe ...... as I find myself moving toward that star in the sky, moving up, and up and up ...... my body feels weightless as it lifts up to the star, going higher and higher, up and up ...... and as the star grows bigger and bigger I realize I am getting quite close to the star ...... closer to its beauty and light ...... as it just gets bigger and bigger ...... brighter and brighter ...... until all at once I am that star in the night sky ...... that beautiful star ...... twinkling away ...... that silver solitary star in the night sky ...... I become the star and the star is me ...... and it's a beautiful star ...... and I find myself drifting deeper and deeper ...... becoming even more deeply relaxed ...... just letting go ...... deeper and deeper ...... into an inner peace ...... as I allow my mind to drift to a special place of comfort ...... as I imagine my perfect place ...... my special place ...... and I can just allow myself to consider how amazing my physical body is ......

...... I become aware that my body is an evolving and changing entity with each and every cell renewing itself hourly ...... daily ...... every day ...... every week ...... and the cells that make up my body today ...... my liver ...... my skin ...... my stomach ...... are not the same cells that existed a month ago ...... they are new ...... fresh ...... perfectly formed cells ...... as my body starts afresh every few hours and days ...... how amazing my body is ...... how strong and solid and permanent my skeleton feels and yet it wasn't there three months ago ...... every cell has been replaced ...... with a new ...... clean ...... fresh cell ...... my body is constantly changing ...... and this allows me to have control over my body ...... because I can influence these new cells ...... I have the opportunity to start afresh every few hours ...... days ...... weeks ...... and months ...... like starting a fresh page ...... allowing myself to feel full of energy ...... well ...... strong ...... alive ......

My body is made up of organs ...... bones ...... skin ...... and muscle ...... but each of these is made up of cells ...... groups of cells each with its own DNA ...... DNA is like the director of a play with each and every cell of my body being the actors ...... the director decides what each cell should be doing ...... how they should be doing it ...... and therefore directs what is going on in the body each and every moment ...... but each actor does not work in isolation ...... each cell receives communication from other cells ......

My unconscious mind can instantly communicate with the trillions of cells in my body ...... everybody's body knows how to heal itself ...... over time ...... broken bones heal ...... cuts and bruises heal ...... effortlessly ...... unconsciously ...... the brain sends out the correct signals to make this happen ...... however, everyday stress ...... can result in the wrong messages being sent ...... resulting in the body becoming out of balance ...... prone to infection or illness ...... but I can re-programme my body ...... here and now ...... today ...... rebalance these imbalances ...... block the wrong messages and send the correct messages ...... renew ...... rejuvenate ...... rebalance ......

And so I will give my unconscious mind an opportunity ...... in this deeply relaxed state ....an opportunity to send out the correct signals ...... to cleanse any toxins and leave only purity ...... to replace tired and worn out cells with clean fresh cells ...... to boost my immune system ...... clearing up any unwanted bacteria or viruses ...... leaving me energized and healthy ......

...... as I experience my immune system working now ......
[IMAGINE your immune system: You may want to see it as an army of strong little fighters, or millions of cells all brightly coloured cascading though your blood, you may feel it as a vibrant energy running through your cells or just as a physical sensation washing over you, you may choose to use your knowledge of white blood cells to form a picture. However you see it, allow the images and feelings to develop.] ...... as I can feel my immune system working inside me

...... cleansing my cells ...... and a feeling of well-being washing over me ...... as I appreciate how good I feel.

...... and I am now so deeply relaxed ...... and comfortable ...... and just enjoying a time when there is nothing of any importance for me to do ...... I can just be ...... and my mind is so receptive to my inner communications that everything I communicate now ...... in this deeply relaxed state ...... will help me in a positive way in my everyday life ...... and as a result of my inner rest and rejuvenation I will feel healthy and full of vitality ...... I will feel confident and optimistic ...... looking forward to things in life ...... but also enjoying the here and now ...... and these good feelings will grow and develop as my levels of confidence increase and I feel really good about myself ...... really enjoying being me ...... when I do resume my normal everyday waking state I will notice that I feel good and have all the energy I need to do all the things I have to do but also all the energy I need to do all the things I want to do ...... as I notice more positive things in life ...... and I will feel confident and optimistic ...... relaxed and calm ......

Only as soon as I am ready ...... and my unconscious mind has finished any processing ...... I will naturally return to a normal alert level of consciousness ...... I will become aware of my physical body ...... as I notice becoming aware of the sounds around me ...... aware of every part of me being awake ...... I am once again becoming aware of where I am ...... and the things around me ...... just as soon as I am ready my eyes will gently open and *every part of me is back here in the present* ...... I am aware of the outside world around me ...... I am aware of feeling great ...... refreshed ...... rejuvenated ...... and so I will just allow my eyes to open as soon as I am ready ...... to just allow my eyes to open ...... gently in my own time ...... feeling refreshed ...... rejuvenated ...... relaxed and calm ...... looking forward ...... feeling positive and full of energy ......

MAIN POINTS
▶ Consider the body renewing itself.
▶ Imagine the communications systems in your body.
▶ Consider how the body heals itself naturally.
▶ Imagine your immune system working effectively.
▶ Communicate positive feelings of well-being.
▶ Return to a normal alert state.

THINGS TO REMEMBER

▶ Stress can have a negative impact on the immune system and health and well-being. Self-hypnosis can be beneficial in reducing stress and the biological consequences of stress.

23

....

Self-hypnosis and weight loss

In this chapter you will learn:
• *techniques for weight loss and for controlling eating patterns.*

Self-hypnosis can be highly effective in helping you to lose weight and control your eating patterns. Weight issues are a result of an interaction between the psychology and the biology of an individual. Self-hypnosis can help you change your thought patterns and behaviours which influence your body. This next section looks at how these techniques work and explains each technique in detail. Provided is a self-hypnosis weight loss plan designed to enable you to lose weight and maintain your ideal body weight long term.

Weight issues

Excess weight is a problem which is growing to epidemic proportions. Recent statistics shows us that 50 per cent of the adult population in the UK are overweight and around 25 per cent are clinically obese. Therefore a quarter of the adult population have a serious condition which impedes their everyday life and may result in poor health and possibly an early death. Obesity results in type II diabetes, heart failure, stroke and a host of other life threatening disorders. It also limits activities and contributes to unhappiness. One of the major issues facing many countries today is the percentage of children who are obese. Recent statistics show that currently around a third of children in the UK are overweight or obese and 70–80 per cent of these children will go on to be obese adults. Weight is often defined in terms of the body mass index (BMI). BMI = weight (kg)/ height (m)^2; a BMI of 19–24 = ideal, 25–29 = overweight, 30+ = obese. Body mass index does not take into account the amount of muscle you have and as muscle is heavier than fat then if you have a high percentage of muscle it is not a true representation.

Insight

Genetics predict about 50 per cent of variation in BMI but weight does not have to follow the patterns of your genes. Your thoughts, beliefs and behaviours all affect your appetite and weight and you can have control over these aspects.

Self-hypnosis can help you control the biological mechanisms within the body to help you maintain a steady and healthy weight. The body is designed to maintain a healthy weight. However, these natural systems may have been damaged and no longer function correctly. Self-hypnosis can help you to control the psychological and biological mechanisms that determine weight. Self-hypnosis can help you to re-set your body, change thoughts and change behaviour to enable you to lose weight and maintain a healthy weight long term.

EAT WHEN YOU ARE HUNGRY

Self-hypnosis can help you learn to recognize when you are hungry. It is important to eat when you are hungry. Dieting damages the biological mechanisms in the body. Dieting in the long term can cause weight gain. Cutting calories to a very low level puts the body into starvation mode where muscle is used to replace energy, rather than fat stores, and the body's metabolism (the rate we use energy in our cells) is reduced to conserve energy. When a normal diet is resumed the body is less efficient. The metabolism of the body is slower so fewer calories can be ingested without further weight gain. Muscle uses up energy. The less muscle you have the less energy you need and therefore the fewer calories you can consume without putting on weight. Yo-yo dieting can result in weight gain in the long term as the body becomes less efficient at using up excessive calories. Often people say if they were the weight they had been when they started dieting they would be happy and wished they had never gone on a diet to start with. People seldom keep off the weight they lose because they haven't tackled the underlying biological and psychological issues.

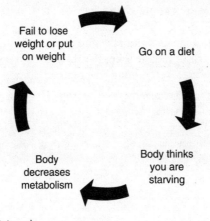

Figure 23.1 *The dieting cycle.*

When you are hungry chemicals are sent to the brain from the gut to encourage food intake. Even though you experience feelings of hunger in your body it is actually the brain that determines hunger. Many of the same messages or signals that are found in the stomach and intestine are also found in the brain. These so-called gut-brain messages can cause or inhibit hunger and affect your appetite. However, if you eat when you are not hungry you are overriding this natural mechanism.

STOP EATING WHEN YOU ARE FULL

Signals of hunger or fullness are dictated, in part, by the number of fat cells in your body. The more fat cells, the more a chemical called leptin is produced by the body. The role of leptin is to send messages to the hypothalamus in the brain to control appetite. The more fat cells you have, the more leptin is produced, the less hungry you should be. This is designed to regulate how much you eat. However, this mechanism may have stopped working efficiently. Overeating and failing to stop eating once you feel full prevents this system from working properly. Self-hypnosis can help you relearn to recognize these physical messages unconsciously so that you will find it much easier to recognize feelings of fullness and will not have the desire to eat more than your body needs.

EAT SMALLER PORTION SIZES

The stomach is an expandable organ and it can become stretched and oversized through eating too large portions. This then causes you to 'feel' hungry in between meals. Luckily it doesn't take too long to return to a healthy size if you cut down your portion sizes. This then encourages the brain to register when the stomach is full and will prevent you from overeating. Having a smaller stomach will prevent you from feeling as hungry and you will be able to eat less and still feel satisfied. Self-hypnosis can help you to change your behaviour to retrain your body. It can also help you with changing your beliefs surrounding food and enable you to feel satisfied with less food.

Cutting down on portion sizes and feeling satisfied eating less food enables you to begin to recognize more easily the signals from your body. Serve yourself half of the amount you would normally eat; if you are still hungry later you can eat more. Remember you are learning to retrain your body and mind to eat only when you are hungry and to stop eating once you are full. Often people are brought up to eat everything on their plate and it is considered polite to leave a clean plate. To encourage children to grow up with a healthy attitude to food, help them learn to recognize their internal signals by letting them finish eating when they report feeling full even if they still have food on their plate.

The social rules of eating can cause us to dismiss the body's signals. Evidence shows that if you deprive someone of their sight temporarily by blindfolding and allow them to eat until they feel full, they eat much less than when they can see the food on their plate. This is because they are purely relying on the physical cues from their body. Your body knows how much it needs to eat to be healthy and you can learn to recognize these signals again.

EAT SLOWLY AND CONSCIOUSLY

Eating slowly helps you to eat consciously. This allows you to re-educate your body. Eating slowly and eating consciously help reinstate the natural mechanism. Self-hypnosis can help you feel satisfied by eating less food and by eating more slowly as you become more aware of your eating and more in control of your body.

It also makes you able to develop a healthy appetite. Your body knows what it requires. You will begin to learn to listen to your body to help you decide what to eat. Research shows that if you allow young children to choose their own food, over a few weeks they naturally choose to eat a balanced diet. Your body naturally knows what it needs and what you should be eating but years of eating for reasons other than hunger have confused your body. Self-hypnosis can help to re-educate your body to regain its natural ability to help you make the right food choices and you will enjoy eating the right food.

Increasing motivation

When deciding to change something in your life in a positive way it is important to consider your motivation. Motivation is key to successful weight loss. What exactly do you want to achieve? It is useful to write down specifically what you want? Some examples may include: to be able to fit into a size 12; to feel you look good naked; to be able to walk up a hill; to enjoy your body; to go on holiday and feel confident in swimwear; to have more energy.

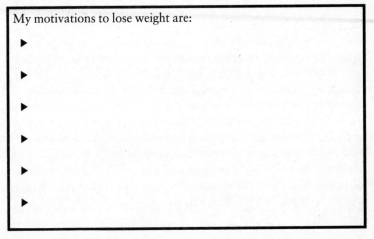

My motivations to lose weight are:

▶

▶

▶

▶

▶

▶

Figure 23.2 Why do I want to lose weight?

These desires and goals can be reinforced with self-hypnosis to increase your motivation.

It is equally useful to consider what may be hindering your motivation. There may be unconscious reasons why being overweight has positive benefits that are protecting you in some way. Once these protective benefits are identified you can easily use self-hypnosis to help your unconscious mind to find new and better ways of coping with these issues. Consider how being overweight may have become useful to you. This is often the most challenging but also one of the most useful psychological strategies to help you to lose weight successfully and can ensure you are fully motivated to lose weight.

There may be reasons why you are not fully motivated to lose weight. Some people identify that being overweight has developed as a protective mechanism. For example, being overweight becomes an excuse for not doing certain things or for not succeeding. For example, one client realized being overweight had been useful because it had enabled her to have an excuse not to go swimming. This was an advantage because she was scared. If she did actually lose weight successfully she would no longer have an excuse and she would have to face up to her fear of water; something she didn't want to have to do. Another woman realized that she used her weight as an excuse not to have sex with her husband. Her lack of libido was a problem she didn't feel she could deal with and therefore it was easier to be overweight and then she didn't have to face up to this problem. In fact her weight may have contributed to hormonal changes in her body causing the lack of libido and losing weight was a solution. Once these women had identified that although they consciously wanted to lose weight unconsciously there might be reasons why they were overweight, they used self-hypnosis to change their thoughts and beliefs. Often just recognizing there are reasons why you may have found being overweight useful and allowing the unconscious mind to reprocess this information whilst in self-hypnosis is helpful. You can realize on an unconscious level that you want to lose weight and that you can lose weight without fear.

Fear is often one of the main reasons people hold onto habits they consciously want to stop. This causes a feeling of helplessness because there is a fear of losing weight and there is a fear of not losing weight. The positive effects of self-hypnosis can naturally lead to a reduction in these negative thought patterns and allow you to be fully motivated to lose weight successfully.

It is useful to write down the reasons that may be maintaining your weight.

Being overweight has become useful to me by:

1.

2.

3.

4.

Figure 23.3 *Why am I maintaining my weight?*

Emotional eating

The part of the brain that controls appetite, the hypothalamus, is also involved in emotion and this is why how much you eat is also affected by your mood.

Often people eat for emotional reasons, as a comfort or when they are stressed or upset. You may recognize this in yourself. Your body gets into the habit of expecting food, usually in the form of carbohydrates or fat, things like chocolate, bread and sweets, when it experiences an emotional episode. This can become habitual. Self-hypnosis can help to break this pattern and retrain your brain not to crave these foods when you feel emotional distress. Some people find that any emotion, whether they feel happy or sad, will cause them to reach for food.

Some people eat when they are upset; some eat when they are bored or when they dislike themselves. Some people eat when they feel guilty, when they are worried or anxious, when they feel unfulfilled. Self-hypnosis can help you to control your stress levels and eating patterns so that you don't automatically reach for food to make you feel better. Most people recognize that eating excessively actually results in only a short-term gain and in the long term actually makes you feel worse – worse about yourself and about your life. On the other hand, eating when you are hungry to give your body the energy it needs to live a full and productive life makes you feel good about yourself.

Change thoughts and behaviours

Self-hypnosis can be very helpful in helping you to change your thoughts and behaviours in relation to food. Slim people tend not to think about food very much. Studies show that people who are overweight tend to think about food more than people of an ideal weight. Self-hypnosis can be of great benefit in retraining your mind not to obsess about food.

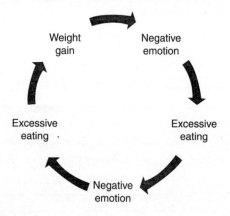

Figure 23.4 The negative spiral of emotional eating.

In addition to self-hypnosis it is useful to keep an emotional food diary if you suspect you eat for reasons other than hunger. Every time you want to eat something, think 'am I hungry?' If the answer if 'yes' then eat and enjoy. If the answer is 'no' then instead of eating write down your thoughts and feelings. Then reassess whether you still feel the need to eat. You will often find that the feeling has passed. Each time you want to eat something when you are not hungry, write down exactly how you are feeling. Remember that this is your private diary and no one else will see it.

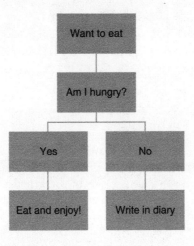

Figure 23.5 *Do I need to eat?*

Control food cravings

Food cravings are very common: surveys estimate that 90 per cent of women and nearly 70 per cent of men report having experienced cravings. Food cravings activate brain areas related to emotion, memory and reward.

Food craving can be controlled with the use of self-hypnosis. During hypnosis the body produces more of a hormone called oxytocin. Oxytocin is produced naturally by the body at certain times; it produces relaxation. Oxytocin has anti-stress properties. It has also been shown to be involved in cravings. An increase in oxytocin reduces cravings. Therefore self-hypnosis can have a direct effect on helping you reduce any food cravings due to the positive effects of oxytocin production.

The insula receives information from other parts of the body and translates those signals into subjective feelings. It is partly responsible for hunger and is involved in food cravings.

Provided below is a complete self-hypnosis script to help you alter your eating patterns, control your cravings, change thoughts and beliefs and alter the way your body responds to food. You can condition your body to lose weight and maintain a healthy weight. You do not need to diet but will you find that you automatically have a different attitude to food.

Script for weight loss

As I make myself comfortable ...... and gently close my eyes ...... remembering this is my time ...... a time for me ...... I just focus on my breathing ...... in and out ...... slowly ...... in and out ...... and as I really focus ...... concentrate on breathing ...... in and out ...... deeper and deeper ...... in and out ...... and as I do I just let ...... the little muscles at the side of my eyes and the sides of my mouth just relax ...... melt away ...... as I become comfortably aware of my whole body relaxing all the way through ...... I only need to relax and let the sounds wash over me ...... there is nothing of importance for me to do ...... just to listen to the sound of my own inner voice ...... which in my own way will help to relax me ...... all the way through ...... relaxed ...... I can forget my physical body ...... and the constraints of my physical self and just allow myself to drift ...... drift wherever my imagination takes me ...... a happy memory ...... a favourite place ...... a dream ...... wherever I go my inner voice will go with me ...... as I drift off ...... floating ......

As I imagine standing at the top of a beautiful staircase ...... a strong staircase with a strong hand rail ...... in a few moments I am going to count down from 10 to 1 and with each number I will walk down one step of the staircase ...... and with each descending number form 10 to 1 I will become 10 per cent or one-tenth more relaxed ...... deeper and deeper ...... All the way down ...... so 10 ...... 9 ...... 8 ...... feeling more and more relaxed ...... 7 ...... 6 ...... 5 ...... 4 ...... 3 ...... 2 ...... all the way down ...... and 1 ...... deep, deeply relaxed ...... I step off the staircase now and find myself in my own special place ...... a place in my imagination ......

And now that I am deeply relaxed ...... I can become fully aware of the aspects of my life I want to change ...... my weight ...... my attitude to food ...... and I can now give myself an opportunity to access my unconscious mind ...... an opportunity to allow my inner mind to identify any emotional issues surrounding my eating ...... just give myself some time ...... and I can give my inner mind a few moments to become fully aware of the positive and protective reasons why I overeat ...... maybe there are some benefits to being overweight that my unconscious mind is aware of ...... that have prevented me from losing weight in the past ...... but I am now ready to overcome ...... and I now have the opportunity to ask my unconscious mind for new and more effective ways of dealing with these issues ...... my old eating patterns served a purpose, but my unconscious mind will find new ways ...... and as soon as my inner mind has found a wonderful new way of coping and responding ...... so that my overeating may soon be viewed as a thing of the past ...... my mind can drift ...... remembering some pleasant memory from the past ...... or a pleasant daydream of the future.

As I find myself so deeply relaxed I know I can become aware of my unconscious mind ...... and let it communicate new thoughts that are good for me ...... and over the next few days I will find it easy to go for hours without thinking about food ...... and if occasionally I find myself thinking about it just for a moment ...... I will quickly and easily find myself becoming absorbed in something else, something more interesting ...... I will find it easy to eat less but still feel satisfied ...... I will feel amazed at how easy it is ...... I feel in control ...... My body will naturally stop eating before I feel full ...... as I am in control ...... I will recognize the feeling of fullness ...... and want to stop eating as soon as I begin to feel full ...... I have waited a long time ...... I don't have to wait any longer to lose the weight I have waited so long to lose ...... and as soon as I reach for something I don't need to eat because I am not really hungry I will find it easy to let go ...... I will automatically just find myself becoming interested in something else ...... and as soon as I even think about food when I am not hungry my mind, from now on, will allow me quickly and effortlessly to think about something else ...... something more interesting ......

...... and so I will begin to notice over the next few days that I feel satisfied with small quantities of food ...... and these small quantities of food will satisfy me completely ...... I will have no desire to eat anything between meals ...... or after my evening meal at night ...... I will have no desire to eat anything until breakfast in the morning ...... the calories in the food that I eat will be completely utilized by my body ...... and not stored as unnecessary fat ...... and I will have new-found energy as my metabolism gains speed ......

With this new pattern of eating ...... and my real desire to lose weight ...... I will find an overwhelming compulsion to think of myself in a positive way ...... deep down inside I know that it is okay for me to do this ...... as I begin to think of myself in better and more positive ways ...... I stop for a moment and think of a time in a few weeks time ...... noticing some amazing changes ...... as I see myself getting more done ...... relationships are working better ...... I am happier ...... more confident ...... I experience a sense of that pleasure now ...... I really feel that pleasure that I have dreamed of ...... I can achieve what I want ...... and I learn to expect more of these good feelings every day ......

And it will be easy ...... so much easier than I ever expected ...... as I have made the mental decision to stop making my life hard for myself ...... I deserve to be happy ...... over the next few hours ...... days ...... and weeks ...... my metabolism will speed up ...... as I picture it now as a small machine inside my body ...... I see its shape ...... hear it turning ...... feeling it deep within me ...... affecting every cell in my body ...... feel it speeding up now as energy races round my body ...... using up more energy ...... supplying me with more energy ...... I really see it whizzing round inside my body ...... picturing the machine with a dial on it and turning that dial ...... turning the dial up ...... as my metabolism speeds up ...... and my mind will continue to help my metabolism to work better and faster over the next few hours ...... the next few days ...... and I am amazed at how much energy I have ...... energy to do things ...... energy to feel good about myself ......

And I now know ...... that I will find it easy to say no ...... when I am full ...... I will know when I am full ...... and when I know I am full ...... I can immediately and easily stop eating ...... as I know now that I am in control ...... in control of my eating ...... in control of my life ...... and as well I notice that I am full of energy and feel really good about myself ...... enjoying being me ......

...... and as each day goes past ...... I will feel physically stronger ...... and fitter in every way ...... I will notice feeling more alert ...... more optimistic ...... more energetic ...... than I have felt in a long ...... long while ...... and as I become more calm and relaxed ......

as each day goes by ...... so I will develop more confidence in myself ...... naturally more self-confident ...... and I will notice a feeling of contentment ......

...... as over the next few days and weeks I will begin to notice a general sense of well-being ...... a satisfaction with life ...... small pleasures in life will please me ...... when I come round from this beautiful state of self-hypnosis I will feel refreshed and invigorated with a sense of inner calm ...... I will automatically eat consciously and only eat consciously ...... and be aware of every mouthful... enjoying every mouthful ...... and feeling the compulsion to stop eating once I feel full ...... I will eat slowly ...... even noticing I put my fork down in between mouthfuls ...... I will only have the desire to eat when I am hungry ...... I will feel amazed at how easy it is ......

And now ...... my unconscious mind has found new and more positive ways of dealing with my emotions ...... recognizing that I no longer need to use food to help control my emotions ...... I am in control ...... I am strong ...... I have developed new strategies ...... excited by the new me ...... the new feelings of confidence I have ...... each and every day growing more and more confident ...... enjoying being me ......

and ...... in future if I find myself upset or angry or bored or emotional ...... I will consciously and immediately focus on positive aspects of my life ...... from now on I will notice how good I feel ...... optimistic and excited about life ...... confident and happier than I have felt in years ...... I now ...... have a relentless passion ...... to achieve my goals ...... I will eat slowly and consciously ...... eat less and feel satisfied ...... I imagine now being in situations when in the past where I have overeaten ...... feeling this calm and relaxed ...... I will assume other people will be thinking good things about me ...... as I feel good about myself ...... happy and confident ...... proud of my new eating habits ......

I can overcome problems ...... my mind can generate creative ways to overcome problems ...... enjoy challenges and realize they make me stronger and wiser ...... I will value my achievements ...... I am here to do something wonderful with my life ...... I am an exceptional person ......

...... I realize that everyone in life performs a role or perhaps many roles ...... mother ...... wife ...... husband ...... friend ...... sister ......

brother ...... work colleague ...... and as I realize that in life we all play different roles ...... in the family ...... at work ...... socializing ...... the funny one ...... the shy one ...... the overweight one ...... it is like wearing a mask ...... and we all wear masks that we have worn for a long time ...... maybe since childhood ...... and although they can be useful ...... they can be outdated ...... and no longer appropriate ...... as I imagine now the mask I commonly wear in life ...... feel it fitting on my face ...... it as I just imagine it there ...... and as I realize that one of the useful things about masks is that they can be taken off and replaced at will ...... and it may be that now ...... is a good time for me to develop a new mask ...... a mask that better represents the new me ...... the slimmer ...... more confident me ...... as I just feel the old mask on my face now and with each out breath it is becoming looser and looser ...... as I begin to feel fresh air flowing over the skin as the mask comes off ...... and as I just place the mask to one side for now ...... and let my unconscious inner mind search for a new mask ...... a new more appropriate mask that suits me now ...... just allowing my mind to find the right one ...... and as I find a new mask and gently place it on my face ...... I realize that masks bring with them feelings ...... thoughts ...... confidence ...... a new role ...... a more appropriate role for me now ...... and I just breathe a little more deeply now ...... as I enjoy the comfortable feeling of my new mask ...... soft and gentle ...... giving me confidence and ease ......

...... and I am now so deeply relaxed ...... and comfortable ...... and just enjoying a time when there is nothing of any importance for me to do ...... I can just be ...... and my mind is so receptive to my inner communications that everything I communicate now ...... in this deeply relaxed state ...... will help me in a positive way in my everyday life ...... and as a result of my inner rest and rejuvenation I will feel healthy and full of vitality ...... I will feel confident and optimistic ...... looking forward to things in life ...... but also enjoying the here and now ...... and these good feelings will grow and develop as my levels of confidence increase and I feel really good about myself ...... really enjoying being me ...... when I do resume my normal everyday waking state I will notice that I feel good and have all the energy I need to do all the things I have to do but also all the energy I need to do all the things I want to do ...... as I notice more positive things in life ...... and I will feel confident and optimistic ...... relaxed and calm ......

Only as soon as I am ready ...... and my unconscious mind has finished any processing ...... I will naturally return to a normal alert level of consciousness ...... I will become aware of my physical body ...... as I notice becoming aware of the sounds around me ...... aware of every part of me being awake ...... I am once again becoming aware of where I am ...... and the things around me ...... just as soon as I am ready my eyes will gently open and *every part of me is back here in the present* ...... I am aware of the outside world around me ...... I am aware of feeling great ...... refreshed ...... rejuvenated ...... and so I will just allow my eyes to open as soon as I am ready ...... to just allow my eyes to open ...... gently in my own time ...... feeling refreshed ...... rejuvenated ...... relaxed and calm ...... looking forward ...... feeling positive and full of energy ......

MAIN POINTS

▶ When in a deeply relaxed state of self-hypnosis become aware of wanting to change your eating behaviour and of your desire to lose weight.
▶ Allow your unconscious mind to acknowledge any reasons that have been stopping you successfully losing weight in the past.
▶ Acknowledge that your eating patterns and weight issues may have been protecting you in the past but that you no longer need them.
▶ Give your unconscious mind an opportunity to find new and more appropriate ways of dealing with issues so that you can successfully lose weight.
▶ Use key positive communications.
  ▶ I will find it easy to go for hours without thinking about food.
  ▶ I will find it easy to eat less and feel satisfied.
  ▶ My body will naturally stop eating when I am full.
  ▶ I am in control of my eating, I am in control of my life.
  ▶ I will naturally eat slowly and consciously.
  ▶ I will only want to eat when I am hungry.
  ▶ Create an image of your metabolism, allow it to speed up.
  ▶ Imagine a mask that represents the old you.
  ▶ Replace it with a new mask.
▶ Communicate positive feelings of well-being.
▶ Return to a normal alert state.

THINGS TO REMEMBER

▶ Weight issues arise due to psychological and biological interactions of the body. Self-hypnosis is a useful tool to help you retrain your body and mind to help you develop a healthier attitude to food and to retrain your body to allow you to lose weight successfully and remain at a healthy weight long term.

24

Self-hypnosis and sleep issues

In this chapter you will learn:
• *techniques to improve the quality of your sleep.*

We are designed to sleep. Humans on average spend nearly 2,500 hours asleep every year. This equates to approximately seven hours sleep a night. People vary in the amount of sleep they require, but good quality sleep is important for psychological and physical health.

Sleep deprivation can lead to cognitive problems, memory loss, an inability to solve simple problems and a heightened emotional state. Poor sleep can lead to increased anxiety and health problems. It can leave you exhausted and lacking in energy which can affect productivity and leave you unable to function at a high level in your waking life. Poor sleep patterns affect the ability to lose weight, and they can contribute to heart disease and high blood pressure and increase the risk of diabetes. Good quality sleep can improve physical health. Powerful antioxidants are produced during sleep which increase immune system functioning.

Insomnia is the most common sleep disorder, affecting approximately 8 per cent of the population. Self-hypnosis is particularly well-suited to help insomnia as it can be practised before sleep as an aid to inducing sleep. Insomnia is an example of the body being out of balance. The balance between the sympathetic and parasympathetic nervous system is not working efficiently. You can retrain this system with self-hypnosis.

Psychology of sleep

When you are asleep the body goes through different stages of sleep.
Initially you enter stage 1 sleep which only lasts a short while and
is just a way of your body entering into a deeper sleep, then stage 2
sleep, which turns into stage 3, and ultimately into stage 4 sleep. You
also have brief periods of REM sleep, in which dreaming takes place.
This whole cycle repeats approximately every 90 minutes in adults.
Children have longer periods of REM sleep than adults and less sleep
is required as you get older.

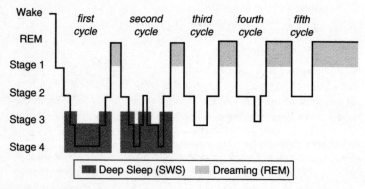

Figure 24.1 The stages of sleep.

Stage 4 sleep is the deepest form of sleep. It is this deep sleep which
has the most benefit for the body and mind. It is the essential part of
sleep. Encouraging your body to enter stage 4 sleep easily is useful
because you can ensure that the sleep you are getting is benefitting
you. From time to time everyone experiences a sleepless night where
you know you must have fallen asleep but it feels as though you were
never really fast asleep and you tossed and turned all night and woke
up feeling exhausted in the morning. This can occur when you remain
in light sleep and do not enter fully into stage 4 sleep. This may be
due to an imbalance in your nervous system due to stress.

Some people experience this every night and it becomes a major
problem in their lives, affecting everything they do. This can
become habitual as the anxiety about whether you will be able to

sleep makes it more likely that you will have problems sleeping. A vicious circle is created whereby the anxiety relating to the problem sustains the problem and causes the sympathetic nervous system to produce chemicals which will make sleep less likely. Self-hypnosis can help to break this vicious circle. The body needs to be in a state of parasympathetic dominance to sleep. The natural mechanisms of the body which induce sleep can become deregulated through stress. Chronic stress can result in the body remaining in a heightened state of sympathetic dominance when you try to go to sleep. This can prevent sleep, even though you are tired. Resetting this system through deliberate facilitation of parasympathetic dominance allows the brain to instigate sleep and encourages deep sleep.

Sleep is governed by the brain and in particular the hypothalamus, the same area which regulates emotions and appetite and which is involved in the production of the altered state of consciousness you experience in self-hypnosis. This allows for direct manipulation of the sleep process. Self-hypnosis allows you to generate the correct brain wave patterns conducive to sleep. Once in this state you can easily drift off to sleep naturally and will sleep deeply and wake up refreshed. This allows you to retrain your body to go to sleep naturally. In self-hypnosis your brain will produce ALPHA waves reflecting a relaxed state and then will naturally produce THETA waves which, with specific techniques to induce sleep, will encourage the brain to produce DELTA waves and you will fall asleep without even realizing it. Naturally.

Self-hypnosis is not only an excellent tool to help sleep problems, like insomnia, but it is also useful in helping you achieve good quality sleep. Sleep quality varies considerably and it is the good quality of the sleep that makes you feel refreshed and full of energy. Self-hypnosis encourages stage 4, deep sleep, which occurs when the parasympathetic nervous system is most dominant. The more stage 4 sleep that occurs during the night, the more rested and refreshed you will feel the next day.

In this technique you are using the natural ability of the body to respond to the imagination as if it were real. Mirror neurons, special cells in the brain, are activated when we think about someone else doing something. Part of this technique involves imagining someone else asleep and this activates the parts of your brain which make sleep more likely. Your body goes into the same state that you imagine someone else's body to be in when they are asleep. You may find you drift off to sleep at any stage in this process. Allow the process to take place naturally. You may never need to follow the whole procedure as you may fall asleep quite quickly.

Script for a good quality sleep

As I am lying comfortably ...... not trying to do anything ...... just allowing myself to be ...... as I focus on the physically sensations in my body ...... resting comfortably here ...... I just close my eyes and become aware of my breathing and I notice that with every breath I can just let go ...... let go of any tension ...... and as I do ...... silently in my head I can just count down from 33 in threes ...... all the way down ...... and with each descending number I feel a deep sense of relaxation spreading down my body ...... starting across my forehead as I imagine a soft wave of relaxation gently cascading down my face ...... all the little muscles around the side of my eyes ...... just let go ...... any tension melting away ...... and my cheeks begin to let go ...... and my nose and mouth ...... relax ...... as I feel the sensations spreading down into my jaw as it just rests ...... as I count down ...... 33 ...... I can just let go even further ...... 30 ...... as the warmth of relaxation spreads down the back of my neck ...... 27 ...... as I relax even deeper ...... as I let the wave of warmth begin to spread down across my shoulders ...... and it feels so good just to let them sink even deeper into the comfort of the bed ...... 24 ...... like a weight has been lifted off my shoulders ...... as I just let go ...... 21 and the warmth spreads down my arms ...... all the way down to my hands ...... 18 and into my fingers ...... as they rest there ...... gently ...... 15 ...... relaxing ...... 12 ...... all the way down 9 ...... and as I realize that every night I can go to sleep ...... sleeping is easy and natural and after a good night's sleep I can awaken ...... refreshed ...... alert ...... and ready to enjoy the day ahead ...... and I realize that I don't have to try and go to sleep ...... I can stop trying ...... as the warmth begins to spread down into my chest and stomach ...... 6 ...... and then starting at the top of my spine ......

it spreads all the way down my back ...... every muscle just letting go ...... 3 ...... down into my hips ...... and down into my lower body ...... the feelings of warmth travelling down ...... o ...... all the way down my legs ...... as they just rest there so comfortably ...... down past o ...... all the way down ...... minus 3 ...... as the warmth spread into my feet ...... and down to my toes ...... minus 6 ...... all the way ...... down ...... and I am only just aware of my body now ...... as my body begins to sleep ...... minus 9 and as I drift off ...... I may even be surprised when I wake up refreshed in the morning ...... how sleep came so naturally ...... minus 12 not even aware of just drifting off into a deep deep sleep ...... minus 15 deep deep sleep ...... minus 18 in the morning feeling so refreshed ...... rejuvenated ...... revitalized ...... minus 21 but for now I can just forget all that and relax ...... minus 24 even more deeply I can just allow myself to drift into a warm and comfortable sleep ...... minus 27 ...... minus 30 ...... minus 33

...... and as I lie here so comfortable and relaxed ...... I can begin to imagine what it is like for someone else to fall asleep and as I do I can see in my mind a person fast asleep in bed ...... and they look so still and comfortable ...... and their body looks so relaxed ...... and I can just imagine what it is like for them to be asleep ...... and as I do I let my mind drift to imagine other people sleeping ...... as I remember seeing a baby sleep ...... as I imagine what it's like to be a baby sleeping so effortless and easily ...... just drifting off to sleep whenever it needs to ...... and I can see a baby there sleeping so peacefully ...... and I can imagine what it's like to be that baby ...... and as I continue to imagine being deeply asleep I realize that the alternative to being asleep is getting up out of this warm, soft, comfortable bed ...... and getting up ...... as I imagine what that would feel like ...... as I imagine feeling the cold air on my body as I get out of bed ...... and it feels uncomfortable ...... and as I imagine myself getting up ...... and walking across the room ...... and I realize that my body would much prefer it if I just carried on lying here ...... and I can just allow myself instead to continue to imagine what it is like to be asleep ...... as I can see again quite clearly in my mind the body of another person sleeping ...... lying so still and peacefully ...... and as I do so I can imagine being that person ...... and just imagine what it would feel like to be deeply asleep ......

▶ Lie comfortably and focus on your breathing.
▶ Do not alter your breathing but be aware.
▶ Communicate relaxation spreading down your body.
▶ Simultaneously count down from 33 in threes.
▶ When you reach zero carry on counting down to minus 33 in threes.
▶ Imagine the image of someone else asleep.
▶ Imagine what it would be like to be that person.
▶ Imagine instead getting up out of your warm comfortable bed.
▶ Realize your body would prefer to be asleep.
▶ Continue to imagine another person asleep and imagine what it would feel like to be deeply asleep.
▶ Allow your body to drift off to sleep naturally.

THINGS TO REMEMBER

▶ Sleep is a biological necessity and good quality sleep is beneficial to psychological and physical well-being. Self-hypnosis offers an excellent tool to help ensure good quality sleep and is also useful for insomnia.

Part 6
Professional hypnotherapy

25

Professional clinical hypnotherapy

In this chapter you will learn:
* *more about professional clinical hypnotherapy and how to access it.*

Clinical hypnotherapy is a scientific, evidence-based psychological therapy which is highly effective in the treatment of a range of psychological and physical issues and symptoms. Clinical hypnosis has been used within the medical field for many years and its use has been approved by the British Medical Association (BMA), the American Medical Association (AMA), and the British Psychological Society (BPS). It is commonly used in the UK National Health Service (NHS) with over 12 per cent of NHS Trusts accessing hypnotherapy services.

Hypnosis is one of the most commonly used therapies, with an estimated 353,000 patients visiting a hypnotherapist annually, resulting in nearly 1.5 million private and NHS appointments every year in England. To meet this demand, more and more sole practitioners and health professionals are being trained in its use.

Clinical hypnotherapy is a psychological therapy which utilizes hypnosis as its main therapeutic tool. The professional clinical hypnotherapist guides you into a state of hypnosis and then uses advanced therapeutic techniques to allow you to deal with more severe issues in your life. A professional hypnotherapist is trained in psychological therapy and the theoretical and practical aspects of hypnosis.

There are two main reasons why it is more appropriate to consult a professional hypnotherapist for some issues rather than using self-hypnosis. First, they are trained and have a wide knowledge and experience of clinical conditions. Second, it is more effective for some conditions for a therapist to guide you through the process of hypnosis. This can allow for therapeutic techniques to be used that you cannot use with self-hypnosis.

Benefits of clinical hypnotherapy

▶ Effective.
▶ Rapid results.
▶ Cost effective.
▶ Safe with no unpleasant side-effects.

Who can consult a clinical hypnotherapist?

Hypnotherapy is suitable and can be beneficial for most people. Very young children, under the age of five or six years of age, may not have the understanding or levels of concentration required to partake in standard hypnotherapy but some therapists have developed specific ways of helping young children which can be useful. Consult a specialist in this area. There is no reason why you should not continue using self-hypnosis or consult a clinical hypnotherapist as you get older and even the very elderly can enjoy the experience and benefit from it. However, anyone suffering from dementia or people with learning difficulties may find difficulty with their understanding or levels of concentration. Hypnotherapy is not suitable for anyone suffering from any form of psychosis (a severe mental illness), personality disorder or epilepsy.

What to expect when consulting a professional hypnotherapist

A professional clinical hypnotherapist will initially take a case history and may ask you to fill in a detailed questionnaire regarding your physical and psychological health in order to gain a thorough understanding of your problem in the context of your life. If you are consulting a professional hypnotherapist about a physical condition they will enquire about previous treatment and diagnosis and prior to any treatment will ask you to gain agreement from your GP or medical doctor. It is essential that underlying serious medical explanations for your problem have either been ruled out or are being treated.

The hypnotherapist will explain the basis of hypnosis and allay any fears you may have. It is important that you have confidence in the therapist and feel comfortable with them. Your goals of therapy and what you hope to achieve will be discussed.

Length of treatment

Hypnotherapy is often rapid in its effectiveness. Generally most hypnotherapy is effective in two or three sessions and sometimes you only need a single session. This is one of the advantages of clinical hypnotherapy as opposed to other psychological therapies which can often take months or even years to help with issues. Most consultations with a clinical hypnotherapist generally last between an hour and an hour and a half.

How much should you expect to pay for treatment?

The cost of clinical hypnotherapy varies according to the location, and the experience and qualifications of the therapist. You are paying for the time and experience of the therapist. Vastly expensive therapy does not guarantee it is good therapy but if you are offered treatment at a very low rate then be cautious. The person may not be sufficiently trained or experienced. Hypnotherapy may also be accessible through private health care providers and financial support for treatment may be accessed through recognized health protection plans.

How to access professional clinical hypnotherapy

Anyone can access a clinical hypnotherapist privately. Historically finding an ethically trained and professional hypnotherapist has been fraught with difficulties. Fortunately things are now changing. Clinical hypnotherapists can now gain equivalent qualifications to other psychology and medical professionals. Some clinical hypnotherapists are trained at degree level and are ethically trained to a high standard. The number of therapists trained at this professional level is increasing.

There is a genuine intention that all hypnotherapists in the future will be required to have professional training. However, presently anyone can promote themselves as a hypnotherapist. There are many people advertising themselves as hypnotherapists and although there are some excellent therapists in practice some do not have adequate training or knowledge. This is likely to change with formal regulation. Currently there are a number of registers which contain lists of therapists. These are not wholly reliable. Individuals with minimal training can register and some registers accept practitioners who have only received training through distance learning, which is inadequate to practise as a therapist. Many advocate non-scientific practices, which may appear mystical and are not psychologically based. The inclusion of these alternative practices does not promote the professionalism of clinical hypnotherapy.

It is therefore necessary to be cautious in choosing a therapist. I would strongly suggest you consult your doctor who will be able to refer you to a professional and ethically trained clinical hypnotherapist. If you wish to access clinical hypnotherapy independently there are a number of considerations to help you choose the highest standard of care.

How to choose a therapist and what to avoid

Clinical hypnotherapists may work full time in clinical practice or may integrate clinical work with research or other academic pursuits. Some integrate hypnotherapy within other psychological therapies and may be trained medical doctors, dentists, nurses, psychologists or counsellors. Some hypnotherapists are specialists in a particular field, for example pain control or working with children.

Qualifications

You should always check the qualifications of a hypnotherapist and make sure they are competent to treat you. You should also check they have professional liability insurance. This is to ensure they are legitimate therapists. No legitimate therapist would work without insurance. The title 'Dr' can only be used if the therapist has completed a PhD, or they are a medical doctor or dentist. If anyone uses this title in other circumstances they are being unethical. Also be wary of therapists who have a string of letters after their name, unless they are recognizable qualifications. The letters BA or BSc are used following an undergraduate degree; this may or may not be in clinical hypnosis. The letters, MA or MSc denote a post-graduate degree, and PhD denotes a higher level post-graduate degree. The letters DipHE, denote a Diploma of Higher Education which is a recognized academic qualification awarded by a university following two years study. A DipHE in Clinical Hypnosis is the standard qualification to look for to be sure the therapist has been ethically and professional trained. A number of universities offer master's or higher degrees in hypnosis. It is important to recognize this is a research degree and does not guarantee any clinical training. A number of independent training organizations currently award their students a diploma but this is not a recognized qualification and any organization can award diplomas. It does not guarantee ethical or professional training.

Although there are a vast number of societies that hold lists of hypnotherapists, purely being a member of a society gives you no guarantee on the level of training and experience of the therapists. Someone can be a member of a society without professional training.

If you believe the therapist has learned their skills through a distance learning course please be very cautious. These are to be avoided – full stop. It is essential that professional therapists have had considerable classroom tuition in the practical and ethical approaches to hypnosis.

Insight

If a therapist seems to be offering you something too good to be true it often is.

Hypnosis is not a cure for all ailments and anyone advertising that they can cure anything with hypnosis is advertising falsely and should be avoided. Also avoid anyone who offers money back guarantees. This is also unethical and is not conducive to successful therapy.

Be wary of anyone offering past life regression. This is not part of the curriculum of professional training in hypnosis and is not a scientific, evidence-based phenomenon. People may have personal experiences that they explain as memories from a past life but there is no scientific evidence supporting this as yet. By all means explore the subject yourself but be aware that there are ethical issues if therapists claim they can regress you to a past life.

IMPORTANT QUESTIONS TO ASK ANY THERAPIST

▶ What level of training have they had?
▶ Have they been trained in the biological and psychological basis of conditions as well as hypnosis?
▶ Have they experience of your particular condition?
▶ If it is a physical condition, ask whether you should seek agreement with your doctor? If they say this is not necessary then they are practising unethically and you should be wary.
▶ How many sessions do they envisage?
▶ Until the therapist has taken a full case history they will not be able to answer this specifically but will be able to give you an average length of treatment in their experience.
▶ How much does it cost?
▶ Do they have professional liability insurance?
▶ Do they adhere to a code of professional conduct?

This is to assess their level of ethical practice.

THINGS TO REMEMBER

▶ Clinical hypnotherapy is a scientific, evidence-based psychological therapy.

▶ Clinical hypnotherapy is a rapid, cost-effective, safe treatment with no unpleasant side-effects.

▶ There are a number of excellent clinical hypnotherapists working in the NHS and privately. However, you still need to be cautious as training and experience vary amongst therapists.

▶ There is now professional training available and the qualifications to look for are DipHE or a BSc in Clinical Hypnosis. This guarantees the therapist has been ethically and professionally trained.

▶ Accessing clinical hypnotherapy through your GP or on personal recommendation is suggested.

26

....

Treatment with clinical hypnotherapy

In this chapter you will learn:
* *some conditions for which clinical hypnotherapy can be effective.*

PROFESSIONAL CLINICAL HYPNOTHERAPY

People access professional clinical hypnotherapy to help them with a psychological or physical issue or as a means of self-development. Do not underestimate the changes that can occur with clinical hypnotherapy. It can have astonishing effects. However, one should recognize that even though there may be a vast array of symptoms which may benefit from hypnosis it should not be considered a panacea for all things. But, if used appropriately it can have profound effects within both psychological and physical health. It can also help you to improve relationships, and excel at work and socially to help you lead a happier and more fulfilled life.

There is a growing body of evidence based on good quality scientific studies supporting the effectiveness of clinical hypnotherapy. However, it should be recognized that research is in its infancy and some evidence is anecdotal. Presented is a range of issues that may benefit from professional clinical hypnotherapy.

PSYCHOLOGICAL ISSUES

Psychological conditions suitable for clinical hypnotherapy include anxiety and stress, habitual behaviour, panic disorder and phobias. There are also more serious psychological conditions that may benefit from clinical hypnotherapy but should only be used in agreement with your doctor. These include post-traumatic stress disorder (PTSD), obsessive-compulsive disorder (OCD), and some forms of depression.

Anxiety and stress

Anxiety is one of the most common reasons why someone visits a clinical hypnotherapist. Anxiety, worry and stress can affect people in many ways and can lead to problems in their everyday lives, at home and at work. It can have a negative effect on health as well as on relationships. Anxiety may be related to a specific event, like exams or passing your driving test, or more generalized, affecting your everyday life. Hypnotherapy is useful for helping people to access their own resources to deal better with problems in their everyday lives. Anxiety and stress are very suitable for treatment with clinical hypnotherapy.

Habitual behaviour

Clinical hypnotherapy can be useful in treating some forms of habitual behaviour, for example nail biting or teeth grinding. These behaviours are carried out unconsciously, without people being aware of doing them, and therefore hypnotherapy can be particularly helpful. It is difficult to change these behaviours consciously because they are unconscious. It is also useful in helping people with other habitual behaviours like smoking.

Smoking cigarettes is highly addictive. The nicotine in cigarettes is addictive. However, smoking is also psychologically addictive. Nicotine only remains in the body for 48 hours and the symptoms of physical addiction lessen quite quickly, but the psychological effects of addiction remain. Cravings are the result of psychological addiction. The area of the brain most involved in the psychological addiction to smoking is the insula. We know this because damage to the insula through a head injury or stroke frequently results in the person having no desire to smoke and they stop smoking immediately. The insula is involved in your ability to imagine what an experience is going to be like. Cravings are a result of imagining the sensations of smoking which make you want to smoke. If the insula wasn't active the cravings would disappear. One of the ways clinical hypnotherapy can help with stopping smoking is through deactivation of the messages sent to and from the insula, which reduces cravings. In order for clinical hypnotherapy to be successful it essential that the individual wants to stop smoking. Hypnosis cannot force anyone to stop smoking if they do not want to. It can, however, also be useful in motivation if someone is considering giving up smoking.

Panic disorders

Panic attacks are anxiety related and may occur only once or recurrently. If someone has recurrent panic attacks they may be diagnosed with pain disorder. Panic attacks involve feelings of intense apprehension which is often sudden and with no awareness of an obvious cause. Hyperventilation often occurs and the person finds themselves breathing very rapidly. Blood vessels to the brain constrict, to counter the effects of over-breathing, which can cause dizziness, blurred vision and confusion. The person can then feel detached from reality, unable to move, and in severe panic a person may experience a crushing sensation in their chest. This can cause further symptoms of panic and a recursive cycle exists. Having a panic attack can be frightening and the person may fear that they are having a nervous breakdown or misinterpret their symptoms as a heart attack. These feelings, which are due to an increase in the sympathetic nervous system, may provoke a strong urge to escape or flee from the place where the attack began. The body also produces large amounts of the hormone adrenalin. This adrenalin causes the physical symptoms to increase.

Clinical hypnotherapy is particularly effective in helping symptoms of panic because it works both on reducing the anxiety and on rebalancing the sympathetic nervous system from which the problems originate.

Phobias

A phobia is an intense fear of something. Phobias can be specific, relating to a specific object, such as the fear of spiders. Phobias can also be process phobias which are the fear of doing something. This can include fear of flying, fear of social situations, and fear of taking exams, or be related to performance anxiety.

Some common phobias include:

- ▶ Acrophobia: fear of heights.
- ▶ Arachnophobia: fear of spiders.
- ▶ Astraphobia: fear of thunder and lightening.

- ▶ Cynophobia: fear of dogs.
- ▶ Ophidiophobia: fear of snakes.
- ▶ Pteromerhanophobia: fear of flying.
- ▶ Trypanophobia: fear of injections.
- ▶ Claustrophobia: fear of enclosed spaces.

There are also some rare and unusual phobias, which include:

- ▶ Anthrophobia: fear of flowers.
- ▶ Arithmophobia: fear of numbers.
- ▶ Chionophobia: fear of snow.
- ▶ Gamophobia: fear of marriage.
- ▶ Genuphobia: fear of knees.
- ▶ Leukophobia: fear of the colour white.
- ▶ Mageirocophobia: fear of cooking.
- ▶ Octophobia: fear of the figure 8.
- ▶ Selenophobia: fear of the moon.

Phobias are acute fear. What is fear? It can be defined as a painful emotion caused by the apprehension of impending danger. Fear is crucial to human existence and serves a useful purpose in protecting us. However, the fear response can become oversensitive and individuals can become overly fearful about things which it is not useful to be afraid of. This is due to an overactive amygdala. Ultimately the person fears fear itself. This can result in chronic anxiety.

Phobias are often the result of a conditioned fear response. The cause of the initial fear may not be known but the result is that the part of the brain regulating the amount of fear you experience, the amygdala, becomes oversensitive and reacts to an innocuous stimulus with a fear response more suitable for a real threat. Around 10–15 per cent of the adult population suffer from some form of phobia. Women are more likely to suffer from phobias than men. Minor phobias may not cause distress in everyday life and do not require treatment. However, severe phobias can result in major problems with everyday living and require professional help.

We are born with a few innate fears that are designed to protect us but most fears and phobias are learnt behaviour. When you have a phobia it becomes impossible to imagine not being terrified of the things you are scared of. This is because your conscious mind cannot think about the object or situation without instigating a series of physical consequences that set off your fear response. Even seeing the word 'spider' for someone scared of spiders will initiate a cascade of physical symptoms, an increased heart rate, clamminess, and the accompanying emotions of fear and unease. This then results in avoidance. Avoidance is an understandable reaction. If something makes you feel fearful and anxious you don't do it. If something makes you scared, you avoid it. However, this avoidance actually exacerbates the problem and can lead to more serious issues. Clinical hypnotherapy can help treat fears and phobias as it can reset your biological response to the 'fearful' object.

SERIOUS PSYCHOLOGICAL CONDITIONS

There are serious clinical conditions that result from extreme anxiety that may also be suitable for professional clinical hypnotherapy. These include obsessive-compulsive disorder (OCD), panic disorder, and post-traumatic stress disorder (PTSD). These are clinical conditions and should only ever be treated by consulting a professional clinical hypnotherapist with agreement from your GP or psychiatrist.

Post-traumatic stress

Post-traumatic stress disorder (PTSD) is an anxiety disorder that can develop after exposure to a terrifying event or ordeal in which serious physical harm occurred or was threatened. Traumatic events that may trigger PTSD include accidents, violent assaults, natural disasters or military combat. Post-traumatic stress disorder is particularly common following war, with 20 per cent of war veterans reporting some symptoms. Emotional or physical trauma can result in cognitive and emotional experiences that persist after the trauma is over. This results in symptoms such as 'flashbacks' where intrusive memories cause the individual to relive the event as if it were recurring, feelings of emotional numbness, and hypersensitivity to stimuli, particularly loud noise. Nightmares and insomnia are other common symptoms.

Post-traumatic stress disorder symptoms result from an overactive adrenaline response, which creates neurological changes in the brain, particularly the amygdala, responsible for fear responses, and the hippocampus, involved in processing memories. These changes mean that the experience is not fully processed and remains active long after the event that triggered the fear. Current advanced techniques in clinical hypnotherapy involve coupling access to the dissociated traumatic memories with positive restructuring of those memories. Hypnosis can be used to help patients reprocess the traumatic experience and reduce spontaneous intrusive recollections. It is essential for you to consult a professional clinical hypnotherapist if you suffer from symptoms of PTSD. Self-hypnosis is not recommended.

Obsessive-compulsive disorder

Obsessive-compulsive disorder is relatively common affecting around 3 per cent of the population. It involves involuntary obsessions and compulsions. Obsessions are recurrent and so are thoughts that persist despite the individual's desire to resist them. Some people also develop compulsions which involve repetitive action that is often performed as a ritual; these frequently involve checking or excessive cleanliness.

The most common anxieties involve:

▶ contamination: dirt, germs, bodily waste, chemicals
▶ mistakes: locks, taps, appliances, paperwork
▶ order: neatness, symmetry, numbers.

The most common actions are:

▶ checking (28%)
▶ washing and cleaning (26%)
▶ repetition of normal activities (11%)
▶ ordering or arranging (6%)
▶ saving or collecting (3%)
▶ mental counting (3%).

It is the uncontrollability of the thoughts and actions which make it so difficult for people. People often develop these symptoms slowly over time, as a way of coping with a particularly stressful event. But then the symptoms themselves become the problem and prevent people from living a normal life. It is also common to experience OCD when suffering from other symptoms such as depression, or phobias.

Obsessive-compulsive disorder is a neurobiological problem with psychological aspects. Research suggests that OCD involves problems in communication between parts of the brain. There are changes in the brain that cause the behaviour and this behaviour is reinforced with negative thought patterns. Due to its serious nature it is essential that you consult a professionally trained clinical hypnotherapist. Obsessive-compulsive disorder is often treated with medication and the use of psychological therapy, usually cognitive behavioural therapy (CBT). In mild cases hypnotherapy may be beneficial as a sole treatment for relieving symptoms of OCD. However, in more severe cases, there is evidence that the use of hypnotherapy in conjunction with CBT and/or medication treatment can produce beneficial effects.

DEPRESSION

Depression can be reactive or endogenous. Reactive depression is in reaction to an event in your life, for example the loss of a loved one or a relationship breakdown. Endogenous depression is a clinical, biological-based condition, due to a depletion of certain chemicals in the brain, most commonly serotonin. It may appear for no obvious reason, although it is likely to be caused by previous stress. Symptoms include a sad, depressed daily mood, a loss of interest in usual activities, difficulties in sleeping, poor appetite and weight loss, loss of energy, and fatigue, and it may lead to thoughts of suicide. Approximately 6 per cent of the adult population suffer from depression and women are twice as likely to report symptoms of depression as are men. Clinical hypnotherapy is only recommended for reactive depression or mild endogenous depressive symptoms or those being controlled with medication, and only in agreement with your medical doctor. It is a serious condition and is only suitable for treatment from a specialist clinical hypnotherapist who is experienced in using hypnosis to treat symptoms of depression.

PHYSICAL CONDITIONS

There is also a range of physical conditions for which clinical hypnotherapy may be used to help control symptoms. Clinical hypnotherapy does not offer a cure of disease but can help to alleviate symptoms, such as pain, and reduce the negative effect stress has on the body.

CHILDBIRTH

The use of hypnosis in labour has been shown to reduce pain and the need for medication. Clinical hypnotherapy is also useful throughout pregnancy and following birth in providing an excellent means of achieving deep relaxation and positive psychological well-being. There are a number of clinical hypnotherapists who specialize in the use of clinical hypnotherapy in pregnancy and childbirth.

EATING DISORDERS

Anorexia

Anorexia and bulimia are serious eating disorders which may have a biological basis. Anorexia is characterized by a drastic reduction in food intake, an intentional loss of weight with an accompanying fear of gaining weight and disturbances in self-perception. A BMI of below 17.5 or 15 per cent below normal weight are considered markers for a diagnosis of anorexia. Amenorrhea, the loss of periods, is common in women suffering from anorexia. It is considered so serious because between 2 per cent and 15 per cent of those who have the condition die as a result of anorexia or complications that arise from anorexia. Anorexia is a serious health condition and although hypnotherapy may be useful in helping recovery it is essential that this is only within a multidisciplinary approach and with full consultation with the medical team.

Bulimia

Bulimia is more common than anorexia, but less life-threatening, with a prevalence rates of between 1 per cent and 3 per cent. Bulimia is characterized by recurrent episodes of binge eating followed by purging, usually vomiting. Binge eating in bulimia can be excessive with people consuming up to 10,000 calories at a time. People may use laxatives or excessive exercise as well as purging to rid themselves of the excessive food. People with bulimia are generally of a normal weight. Bulimia is diagnosed if a person shows recurrent bulimic episodes over a period of three months, a lack of control over eating, behaviour designed to avoid weight gain, and a persistent and exaggerated concern about weight. Symptoms of bulimia can be helped with clinical hypnotherapy. Consult your GP who may be able to refer you to a specialist.

IRRITABLE BOWEL SYNDROME

Irritable bowel syndrome (IBS) is one of the most common disorders of the digestive system and affects around 1 in 10 people. It is twice as common in women as men. In IBS the bowel becomes supersensitive and responds with violent contractions or spasms to stimuli such as stress or simply eating a meal. Symptoms vary between individuals, but common symptoms include abdominal pain and discomfort, abdominal contractions, spasms or cramps, diarrhoea, constipation, bloating, nausea and indigestion. It is important to consult your doctor if you suffer severely with any of these symptoms as they can be caused by other more serious medical conditions. If your doctor diagnoses IBS then they can refer you for clinical hypnotherapy. The UK's National Institute for Clinical Excellence (NICE), which makes recommendations to the NHS, has approved hypnotherapy as a treatment for refractory IBS. A recent review of all clinical trials using clinical hypnotherapy for IBS concluded that hypnosis produced significant results for reducing IBS symptoms in the majority of participants.

PAIN

Clinical hypnotherapy can be beneficial in treating both acute and chronic pain. Pain can be a sign of a serious health problem and therefore it is important for you to seek advice from your doctor before consulting a professional clinical hypnotherapist. They will be able to advise you and refer you to an appropriate specialist clinical hypnotherapist. General practitioners are very receptive to the use of hypnotherapy to help with reducing the symptoms of pain as they are aware of its benefits. Recent evidence shows hypnosis can help relieve pain in 75 per cent of the population. Clinical hypnotherapy has been shown to be useful in migraines, burns, childbirth, dentistry and minor procedures. There is also evidence that major procedures such as operations can be carried out without the need for analgesia with the use of hypnosis. This is still relatively rare and it may be that some people are particularly receptive to this form of pain relief.

During hypnosis there is a suppression of neural activity which inhibits the emotional interpretation of sensations such as pain. During hypnosis the parasympathetic nervous system is dominant and this reduces pain as fewer pain messages are sent to the brain. Specific techniques are also used to help control the perception of pain. Research has shown that the brain areas that are active when pain is experienced can be deactivated when a patient uses hypnosis to alter their pain perception. Pain is purely a process initiated by messages sent to the brain. If you can alter these messages then less pain is experienced.

PALLIATIVE CARE

Clinical hypnotherapy is used within palliative care, a specialist area of health which focuses on relieving and preventing the suffering of patients in any stage of a disease. This may include undergoing treatment for curable illnesses, and people living with chronic diseases, as well as those nearing the end of life. Palliative medicine uses a multidisciplinary approach to patient care, relying on input from doctors, nurses, psychologists and other allied health professionals. Clinical hypnotherapists work alongside other health professionals in helping people with both terminal and chronic illness. It is used in hospices, care homes and hospitals. Hypnosis has been shown to be useful in helping people with nausea and vomiting resulting from chemotherapy and studies show that many patients feel that hypnotherapy has helped them cope with their illness. It is also useful in controlling and coping with pain. Some centres also recognize the benefits of clinical hypnotherapy in helping relatives and carers cope with the difficulties of looking after someone who is ill or helping them with grief.

SKIN DISORDERS

Clinical hypnotherapy can be effective in treating warts, dermatitis, eczema and psoriasis in both adults and children. Skin disorders are an example of a physical condition with psychological components. They can often be exacerbated by stress because of the biological consequences of stress on the body.

TINNITUS

Tinnitus is the perception of sound in the ear in the absence of corresponding external sound. It is described as a ringing sound or a buzzing noise. Tinnitus is a symptom which can occur due to noise-induced hearing loss, following a sustained loud noise, as a result of an ear infection or as a side-effect of some medication. It is irritating and interferes with sleep and quiet activities, causing severe distress. Sufferers feel anxiety and frustration because it is most problematic when they are trying to relax. It is relatively common particularly in people over 55 with 1 in 10 people in this age group reporting some symptoms of tinnitus.

The symptoms may originate from short-term ear damage because the brain becomes attuned and attention becomes focused on hearing. The brain can perceive noise as a threat, and anxiety becomes attached to the noise. The more someone tries to ignore it the more anxious they become. Clinical hypnotherapy can be useful in helping sufferers to redirect their attention and in reducing the anxiety attached to the condition.

WEIGHT ISSUES

Clinical hypnotherapy is beneficial in losing weight and sustaining a healthy weight long term. You can use self-hypnosis, go to see a clinical hypnotherapist for individual sessions, or join a hypnotherapy weight loss programme where hypnotherapy is conducted as part of a group with additional psychological help and support.

CLINICAL HYPNOTHERAPY IN MEDICINE

Professional clinical hypnotherapy has a wide range of applications in medicine. Hypnosis is increasingly being used within the NHS to help both children and adult patients prepare for and undergo certain medical and dental procedures such as dental extractions, medical imaging scans (CT/MRI), needle phobia and surgery.

Recovery and rehabilitation

Clinical hypnotherapy is one of the most beneficial non-invasive therapies for enhancing the healing of tissues, boosting the immune system and enhancing rehabilitation following injury. There are a number of specialists working in this field.

SELF-DEVELOPMENT

Clinical hypnotherapy can be useful in enhancing well-being and in helping you at work, socially and in relationships. You may also choose to consult a clinical hypnotherapist, not because you have a problem, but purely as a way of enhancing your life. Musicians, writers, artists, and dancers have found clinical hypnotherapy beneficial to help them to tap into their creative resources.

PERFORMANCE ENHANCEMENT

People often choose to consult a clinical hypnotherapist to help them to perform better. Performance can refer to a specific goal, like passing your driving test or doing a presentation at work. It also relates to everyday life: performing well and excelling at everything you do, being confident and successful, whether this is in sport, work, hobbies or relationships.

Optimum performance can be enhanced with clinical hypnotherapy as well as being beneficial in helping you combat any negative effects of nerves and anxiety. Clinical hypnotherapy can be useful in preparation and in the lead up to a performance. You can also learn specific techniques to use during performance and following performance. It is utilized in sport to help athletes to perform to the best of their ability.

The role of anxiety in performance
Anxiety can prevent you from performing at your best and can detrimentally affect your confidence. Anxiety is a physical state. This physical state can be adjusted with hypnosis to help you attain the correct level of stimulation to enhance your performance. It can also make available unconscious resources to help you perform with more confidence.

When in a state of high anxiety, the part of the brain responsible for fear, the amygdala, is overactive. Anxious thoughts, beliefs and emotions produce a whole host of chemicals in the brain which send messages for your body to go into sympathetic dominance; the 'flight or fight' response. In fact it can be useful to your performance to be in a slightly increased state of sympathetic dominance as this heightens your ability to focus. However, when highly anxious you tend to focus internally on the anxiety. You may build up an image of failure and become even more anxious. You may remember previous negative experiences which reinforce your anxiety. You may avoid the situation which only maintains your perceived inability to cope with the experience. You begin to fear the fear.

Clinical hypnotherapy can help you to achieve a more appropriate state which enables you to perform without excessive anxiety. When someone is confident, their state of mind is externally focused on what they are actually doing. Positive thoughts broaden thinking. It is appropriate to feel a level of excitement when performing and this slightly heightened state enables you to perform better. With self-hypnosis you can retrain your mind and body to interpret the physical sensations you experience as excitement as opposed to fear. This allows you to use the adrenalin in your body rather than it working against you.

HYPNOTHERAPY AND CHILDREN

Clinical hypnotherapy is appropriate for use with children. A number of clinical hypnotherapists in the NHS specialize in clinical work with children. Hypnosis is being used successfully in hospitals to help children prepare for surgery. Clinical hypnotherapy is also appropriate for the treatment of nocturnal enuresis (bed wetting) in children. Childhood anxiety disorders can also benefit from clinical hypnotherapy.

THINGS TO REMEMBER

► Professional clinical hypnotherapy is a useful treatment for a range of psychological and physical symptoms.

► Always consult your GP regarding physical symptoms prior to treatment.

► In the near future clinical hypnotherapy is likely to be offered as part of a multidimensional approach within health care.

► Clinical hypnotherapy is also particularly useful in self-development and to enhance performance.

Training in clinical hypnotherapy

In this chapter you will learn:
- *how you can train to be a clinical hypnotherapist.*

Academic developments in the profession of clinical hypnotherapy

Clinical hypnosis is an area of scientific study and clinical application worthy of recognition as an academic subject in its own right. It has strong links to psychology and some undergraduate psychology degree programmes include hypnosis within their curriculum. However, understanding the theoretical basis of hypnosis is not sufficient to be proficient in its clinical applications and therefore it is necessary to offer extensive training both in the theory and practice, as well as gaining clinical experience.

Training in clinical hypnotherapy has fundamentally changed in recent years. The profession of clinical hypnotherapy has been recognized in the larger academic community with the provision of an undergraduate degree in clinical hypnosis. The BSc (Hons) programme provides students with a recognized higher education academic qualification in clinical hypnosis. It combines practical, academic and vocational components to ensure that therapists are appropriately, ethically, and professionally trained.

Historical process

Clinical hypnotherapy has long been recognized as a useful tool with many applications. However, its use has been hampered by poor regulation, and the lack of a validated training route. As with other professions it is necessary that therapists are academically and clinically trained. Academic and clinical training is combined for most health professions, including doctors and nurses. This is now the case for clinical hypnosis training. The development of an academic curriculum ensures that clinical hypnotherapy develops further as a recognized scientific subject area. This is promoting research and therein enhancing clinical work. Clinical efficacy is assessed through research. This can help to develop the most effective techniques to help the range of conditions that respond to treatment with clinical hypnotherapy. As well as extensive practical training, therapists are often trained in the scientific methods of research. This promotes good quality clinical research, providing scientific evidence supporting the use of clinical hypnotherapy. More and more research is being conducted and the medical profession is keen to integrate this knowledge into mainstream health care. This is becoming more viable with professional training and an increase in good quality research.

Standards of training

Degree programmes are written and developed by leading academics and clinicians in the field. All degree programmes undergo a rigorous process of external scrutiny during development, and continuous monitoring to ensure quality of teaching and assessment. This ensures standards across institutions. A UK university degree is a recognized and highly valued qualification all over the world.

Studying for a degree in clinical hypnosis

Presently in the UK, St Mary's University College in Twickenham, London, is the only higher education institution that offers an undergraduate degree in clinical hypnosis. The BSc (Hons) offered by St Mary's in collaboration with the Brief Strategic Therapy and

Clinical Hypnosis (BST) Foundation is the 'gold standard' training for professional hypnotherapists. Other universities will offer undergraduate programmes in the next few years. Some universities already offer master's degrees. These are research degrees taken following completion of an undergraduate degree and do not teach clinical skills. For example, a psychologist may undertake a master's degree in hypnosis in order to conduct research in the field but does not have the clinical skills or knowledge to practise therapy.

St Mary's University College and the BST Foundation are leading the way in academic training through a Centre of Excellence in Clinical Hypnosis. This encompasses a research centre and a clinic, staffed by professional trained clinical hypnotherapists and accessible by self-referral or GP referrals. The Centre offers expert advice and consultation to other academic institutions developing validated programmes in clinical hypnosis. St Mary's University College is working with the Department of Health and other government bodies in ensuring the continuing professional development of clinical hypnotherapy. This work includes integrating clinical hypnotherapy into mainstream primary care and providing GPs and other health care professionals with routes to facilitate referrals.

Who is suitable for training?

Many people consider training in hypnotherapy either as an addition to existing skills, for example, psychiatrists, doctors, dentists, anaesthetists, pharmacists, nurses, psychologists, therapists and teachers. In addition, individuals looking for a rewarding career or a new career path may choose to train as a clinical hypnotherapist. When embarking on training to be a professional clinical hypnotherapist it is not essential to have a prior professional background as the extensive training enables you to progress from a novice to a competent therapist. Clinical hypnotherapy is now a first choice profession for a growing number of people who recognize its therapeutic benefits and understand its biological and psychological foundations. It can provide a fascinating and rewarding career.

Academic study and professional training requires a certain level of competence in verbal and written skills. There is no age limit to training to be a hypnotherapist and it is often something people come to later in life. In fact it is recognized that many people decide to train in hypnotherapy as mature students and do not necessarily have traditional academic qualifications. Applications are dealt with on an individual basis.

Curriculum

A degree curriculum ensures a modern understanding of the psychological and biological aspects of symptoms as well as a theoretical and practical knowledge of hypnosis and its applications. This allows for a broader understanding of possible psychological and biological aspects relevant to therapy and enables the therapist to educate the client prior to specific hypnotherapeutic interventions. This is conducive to effective therapy. The curriculum also ensures that therapists work within clear ethical guidelines with regard to the application of hypnosis and have a full understanding of its limitations as well as its benefits.

The Diploma of Higher Education (DipHE) in Clinical Hypnosis, awarded on successful completion of Level 2 of the BSc, is deemed the appropriate qualification to practise as a clinical hypnotherapist in the UK. A fast-track option enables currently practising therapists, who can provide sufficient evidence of appropriate prior learning, to enter the programme at Level 2. This facilitates experienced therapists to update their training to the appropriate standards easily and effectively. In time it is likely that all clinical hypnotherapists will be qualified to this level.

The full BSc is a three year course. All lectures take place on interspersed Saturdays to allow those working to attend. Levels 1 and 2 provide the student with the theoretical knowledge and clinical skills necessary to practise. On successful completion of Level 2 (240 academic credits) students are considered proficient to practise and can call themselves clinical hypnotherapists and can use the letters DipHE after their name. Level 3 focuses on research methods and all students conduct independent scientific research. This is necessary to gain a full degree and is producing ethically trained therapists with clinical skills, theoretical knowledge and research skills.

Throughout the degree course students learn clinical and therapeutic skills as well at the biological basis of hypnosis and the aetiology of a range of common conditions suitable for treatment with hypnosis.

The BSc in clinical hypnosis is validated:

- ▶ to provide scientific, evidence-based training in clinical hypnotherapy
- ▶ to provide vocational training that develops practical and theoretical skills necessary to become an ethical and professional therapist
- ▶ to provide a scientific understanding of mind, brain and behaviour in relation to hypnotherapeutic methods
- ▶ to provide ethical training in recognizing the limitations of hypnosis
- ▶ to stimulate, encourage and develop students' acquisition and knowledge of a range of therapeutic methods
- ▶ to develop an understanding of the role of empirical evidence in the creation and constraint of theory and of how theory guides therapeutic practices
- ▶ to enable students to understand and appreciate real-life applications of theory in relation to the full range of experience and behaviour
- ▶ to develop knowledge leading to an ability to appreciate and evaluate critically research findings, theory and clinical applications
- ▶ to train students in research methods and statistics
- ▶ to develop students' ability to design and carry out research in the field of clinical hypnosis
- ▶ to develop students' capacity to become reflective and autonomous learners.

Funding

Tuition fees are considerably lower for the BSc in Clinical Hypnosis than for other degrees because of its vocational nature. Please visit www.hypnosistrainingcourses.co.uk for current course fee information. Students on the degree programme can apply for a fee grant and course grant based on their household income. This provides financial help towards the cost of tuition fees and other study costs, such as books, materials and travel. Any financial help through the fee grant or course grant does not have to be paid back. In addition, from September 2012, students will be able to apply for a Tuition Fee Loan. This will not be dependent on household income. This is repaid and graduate students start paying back the loan when they earn over a certain amount.

If you are disabled or you have a specific learning difficulty, you may be able to get extra help through Disabled Students' Allowances. If you have children, or there's an adult who depends on you financially, there may be extra help available, for example, through the Childcare Grant or Adult Dependents' Grant. For current information on applying for grants and loans see www.direct.gov.uk

It is also possible to apply for a Professional and Career Development Loan. A Professional and Career Development Loan is a bank loan. You make an agreement with a participating bank to borrow an amount between £300 and £10,000. Then once you've stopped studying, you pay it back in the normal way. The difference with a Professional and Career Development Loan is that the Young People's Learning Agency (YPLA) pays the interest on the loan while you're studying, and for one month afterwards. After this, you'll pay interest at the rate fixed when you took out the loan. Interest rates on the loans are set so they're competitive with other 'unsecured' personal loans that are commercially available. Currently, banks offer Professional and Career Development Loans at a reduced customer rate. For further information, consult the participating banks.

Professionalism

The advancement in professional training is of benefit to the general public and therapists. It is hoped in time that anyone practising hypnosis in a therapeutic setting will be required to be trained to a professional standard. The effectiveness of clinical hypnotherapy is recognized within mainstream medicine and is becoming integrated into primary care in a way that will allow for greater access to this effective therapy, and will give the general public confidence.

Professionalism is paramount to ensure:

- greater accessibility to the general public
- high standards of care
- progression of clinical research to provide scientific evidence to support clinical practice.

Setting up in practice

Once trained as a clinical hypnotherapists many therapists set up in private practice. Clinical hypnotherapists also work within the NHS and the number of these positions is likely to increase with the new professional standards of training. They continue to develop skills with an on-going programme of professional development.

Ethics

Clinical hypnotherapy is a profession and therefore all ethically training hypnotherapists work according to professional standards. Professional clinical hypnotherapists work within a Code of Conduct including:

- confidentiality
- proper conduct
- working with integrity, impartiality and respect
- recognizing the boundaries of one's own competence
- only working within one's level of competency and experience
- accurate representation of qualifications
- respecting the integrity of other recognized health care professionals
- ensure treatment is concluded at the earliest opportunity
- not bringing the profession into disrepute by engaging in unethical practices.

Professional liability insurance

All therapists are required to have professional liability insurance.

THINGS TO REMEMBER

▶ Training in professional clinical hypnotherapy is becoming more widely available.

▶ A degree programme BSc (Hons) is offered.

▶ Students are proficient to practise following completion of Level 2 on the award of a Diploma of Higher Education (DipHE).

▶ Research and professionalism is being enhanced.

▶ Clinical hypnotherapy offers a rewarding and interesting career.

Glossary

Adrenal glands glands situated above the kidneys, which secrete adrenalin and other hormones

Amygdala areas in the brain concerned with processing memories of emotional reactions

Antioxidants molecules that prevent oxidation and protect the cells from damage caused by free radicals

Autonomic nervous system part of the nervous system that acts unconsciously to control heart rate, digestion and other body processes

Body Mass Index measurement of body fat based on an individual's weight divided by the square of his or her height

Brain complex structure located in the head and protected by the skull; controls all organs and body systems and is in control of the nervous system

Brain stem located in the posterior part of brain; regulates the central nervous system and the sleep cycle

Cerebellum area of the brain involved in movement and balance; crucial in attention and memory, language and mental imagery

Cerebral cortex area of the brain that plays a key role in thought, memory and consciousness

Cingulate gyrus area of the brain that is part of the limbic system; concerned with emotional behaviours

Circadian rhythms changes that follow a roughly 24-hour cycle

Cognitive processing mental process of knowing and awareness

Conscious fully aware or awake; intentional

Consciousness state of being awake and aware of one's surroundings

Corpus callosum band of white matter connecting the two hemispheres of the brain

Cortisol a hormone produced by the adrenal glands in response to stress and to low blood sugar

Diabetes a disorder of metabolism leading to high blood sugar

Dopamine an important neurotransmitter essential for healthy functioning of the central nervous system

Electroencephalography (EEG) technique for recording electrical impulses from the brain

Frontal lobe the anterior area of the brain, responsible for speech, control of skilled movements, mood and personality

Heart failure a term used when the heart becomes less efficient at pumping blood round the body

Hemispheres literally, half a sphere; often used to refer to the two regions of the brain (left and right hemispheres) or the two halves of the world (northern and southern hemispheres)

Hippocampus part of the limbic system, responsible for storing and retrieving memories; essential in processing new conscious memories

Homeostasis the ability of an organism to maintain internal equilibrium

Hormones substances produced in one part of the body that travel to other parts via the bloodstream and affect activities such as growth, fertility, or metabolism

Hyperventilation breathing too fast or too deeply

Hypnosis a state of relaxation or altered consciousness in which deeper parts of the mind become more accessible

Hypnotherapy treatment of a variety of conditions by hypnosis

Hypothalamic pituitary adrenal (HPA) axis a linked system of the body that maintains basal and stress-related homeostasis

Hypothalamus part of the brain that regulates temperature, metabolism and other bodily processes

Immune system collection of organs, tissues and cells that together defend the body against disease

Insomnia inability to fall asleep or stay asleep for an adequate length of time

Insula a region of the cerebral cortex responsible for higher mental functions

Kinesthetic concerning the sense of bodily orientation and touch

Leptin hormone involved in the regulation of appetite

Lethargy state of listlessness or sluggishness

Limbic region group of brain structures involved in emotion and motivational behaviour

Metabolism chemical processes occurring within the cells that are necessary for life

Neurological concerning the nerves or nervous system

Nicotine addictive and poisonous substance found in the tobacco plant

Obesity condition in which excess body fat has accumulated and may affect health

Occipital lobe posterior area of the brain containing visual centre of the brain

Parasympathetic nervous system one of the two divisions of the autonomic nervous system

Parietal lobe upper middle lobe of each hemisphere of the brain; concerned with sensory information such as touch, taste, temperature and with movement

Pituitary gland at the base of the brain which co-ordinates the activities of many other glands

Placebo sham therapy or medication which the patient believes will make him or her well

Positive Psychology a branch of psychology that focuses on improving mental functioning above that of normal mental health by understanding what makes human beings happy and fulfilled

Psychology scientific study of the human mind and behaviour

Psychoneuroimmunology study of the interaction between mental processes and health

Rapid eye movement (REM) REM sleep is the fifth and last phase of the sleep cycle; most dreams occur during REM sleep

Science the systematic study, description and theoretical explanation of phenomena in the physical universe and the laws governing it

Self-hypnosis act of administering hypnotic procedures on one's self

Serotonin chemical neurotransmitter; low levels are associated with mood disorders

Stress body's reaction to changes requiring a response

Stroke sudden death of brain cells due to lack of blood

Sympathetic nervous system one of the two divisions of the autonomic nervous system

Temporal lobe lateral region of the cerebrum, associated with smell, memory and learning

Thalamus oval area of grey matter that relays nerve impulses to other parts of the brain

Unconscious lacking awareness, unresponsive

Taking it further

Sternberg, E. M. (2001) *The Balance Within: The Science Connecting Health and Emotions*, New York: W. H. Freeman.

This is a beautifully written book offering a clear scientific-based explanation for the connection between emotion and health. I recommend anyone interested in mind–body medicine to read this. It is one of my favourite books.

Index

Image credits